EIGHTH DAY PRAYERS

DAILY MERCY FOR LENT AND EASTERTIDE

Sally Breedlove, Willa Kane,
Madison Perry, and Alysia Yates

Forefront
BOOKS

Eighth Day Prayers: Daily Mercy for Lent and Eastertide

Copyright © 2025 Sally Breedlove, Willa Kane, Madison Perry, and Alysia Yates. All rights reserved. No part of this book may be used or reproduced by any means, graphic, electronic, or mechanical, including photocopying, recording, taping, or by any information storage retrieval system without the written permission of the authors except in the case of brief quotations embodied in critical articles and reviews.

This book is a work of nonfiction. Unless otherwise noted, the author and the publisher make no explicit guarantees as to the accuracy of the information contained in this book, and in some cases, names of people and places have been altered to protect their privacy.

Unless otherwise noted, Scripture quotations are taken from the ESV® Bible (The Holy Bible, English Standard Version®), © 2001 by Crossway, a publishing ministry of Good News Publishers. Used by permission. All rights reserved. The ESV text may not be quoted in any publication made available to the public by a Creative Commons license. The ESV may not be translated in whole or in part into any other language. Used by permission.

Scripture quotations marked MSG are taken from *The Message*. Copyright © 1993, 1994, 1995, 1996, 2000, 2001, 2002, 2018. Used by permission of NavPress Publishing Group.

Scripture quotations marked NIV are taken from The Holy Bible, New International Version®, NIV®. Copyright © 1973, 1978, 1984, 2011 by Biblica, Inc.® Used by permission of Zondervan. All rights reserved worldwide. www.zondervan.com. The "NIV" and "New International Version" are trademarks registered in the United States Patent and Trademark Office by Biblica, Inc.®

Cover image & Eighth Day emblem design: Isabel Yates

Library of Congress Control Number: 2024918815

ISBN: 978-1-63763-323-6
E-book ISBN: 978-1-63763-324-3

Published by Forefront Books, Nashville, Tennessee.
Distributed by Simon & Schuster.

Cover Design: Jonathan Lewis
Interior Design by Bill Kersey, KerseyGraphics

Dedication

For Lekita Essa, widowed young, who turned grief into
a way to love others. She heard the Holy Spirit's call
to prayer and shared it with an anxious world.

And for Beatrice Rose Dasher, whose brief eighty-eight
days helped those who knew her steadfast peace
learn to hope in the resurrection of the body
and the life of the world to come.

Contents

Introduction
MADISON PERRY

*W*HAT DAY IS IT? No matter the week or season, there is another name for the day we are living: the eighth day. Jesus Christ was resurrected the day after the last day of the week. If the first day was a day of creation, the eighth day was one of new creation and life in Christ on the far side of the grave. By the power of the Holy Spirit, we can join Christ and live in this new day, even in the midst of the old order.

This book is an invitation to live like eighth-day people. We are invited to a banquet, to feast in the halls of Zion and dwell forever in the kingdom of God. At this table lies nothing less than everything, no matter what we have lost or suffered, or even what we have inflicted on the world around us.

This invitation is present on every page of the Bible. However, left to our own devices, we do not have eyes to see God's glory or ears to hear God's call. Adrift in the imagination of our hearts, we wander through the ruins of another age.

How do we enter this realm of God's resurrection glory? By the work of the Holy Spirit through God's Word. His Word is living and active, capable of piercing even to the dividing of soul and spirit, and his mercies are new every morning.

You likely recognize that you are in the same decaying world that we all experience, where our sense of history comes from the news cycle and to-do lists. This is the stale kingdom of the age that is passing away. What will quicken our hearts, rebuild our imaginations, and pull us back toward our God on a daily basis? Surely God's Word is up to the challenge.

Within *Eighth Day Prayers* you will find passages of Scripture that pull you into the world of God's Word, new landscapes of fresh truth where the Holy Spirit will equip you for friendship with God. We hope that this book moves you to engage with Scripture and that our words will recede into the background, leaving you open to God's Word and its power. We cannot set the terms of your engagement with God, but we hope to guide you into what may feel like new terrain and prepare you for real life—life with Christ.

We have ordered *Eighth Day Prayers* to follow the church's calendar, and the newly revised format comprises three volumes: the Incarnation Cycle contains Advent, Christmas, and Epiphany; the Paschal Cycle contains Lent, Holy Week, Easter, and Pentecost; and the final volume contains Ordinary Time. Each season begins with a brief introduction, and we have added a calendar at the beginning of each page for your convenience. Following the church's calendar will give you the opportunity to connect your daily exposure to God's Word with the expansive story of God's redeeming work. Here we find an older, truer way of living, one that draws its momentum from the arc of salvation and discovers deep wells of rest and strength in Christ.

As you immerse yourself in the Word of God, open yourself to his Spirit, and orient yourself within the life of Jesus, we pray that you will move into a new and richer reality. The kingdom of God is near. Repent, believe, and find your life in the gospel!

Entering In
STEPHEN A. MACCHIA

*T*HE BEST PART OF CONVERSATION WITH FRIENDS is the give-and-take—we don't already know what they are going to say. We notice things about them that we enjoy even as we converse. We are curious, we ask questions, we share real things. We listen intently because the person matters to us. They are not a book we have already read; they are not present merely to tell us what to do or what is wrong with us. They want to know us, and we want to know them.

The ancient practice of *lectio* is like that—it's listening to God's Word, listening to what arises in our hearts as we hear God's Word, and responding in prayer to the Author of these words with real words of our own. *Lectio* is conversation between the triune God and us, the children he so deeply loves, in the context of his beautiful Word.

Consider these ancient words used to describe this way of being with God during lectio:

- We pause for silence and still our hearts to receive God's Word (*silencio*).
- We receive a sacred reading of the text (*lectio*).
- We notice a particular word or image that has leapt off the page into our hearts, and we meditate on that word or image (*meditatio*).
- We prayerfully respond to what we notice stirring in our own heart (*oratio*).
- We linger in silence, noticing more deeply how this particular Scripture is speaking to us (*contemplatio*).
- We say yes to the transforming work God is seeking to do in us as we hold this word from him. How is our soul being nourished and transformed? How are we called to be and what are we called to do in this world (*incarnatio*)?

In many ways this book is designed to guide you into a time of lectio so you can focus on a small portion of God's Word and enter into a prayerful encounter with the living God. When Bible reading becomes prayer, you know you've touched a nerve the Spirit is inviting you to consider. There is a fresh wind of God's Spirit when we genuinely receive the living Word, and it is profoundly good for our souls.

You are blessed to be holding this resource in your hands. May the words of your mouth and the meditations of your heart be inspired by the Word and then multiplied in your soul and in service to others. Receive what God has in store for you like you've never heard the Word before. Such joy!

Introduction to the Christian Year
STEVEN E. BREEDLOVE

*F*ROM THE MOMENT GOD CREATED THE WORLD, he rooted it in time. The six days of creation are endowed with beauty, meaning, and purpose, leading us to the seventh day of divine rest. But what of the eighth day? For Christians the eighth day is the day of Jesus's resurrection from the dead—Easter—on the first day after the Jewish Sabbath. The eighth day marks a new way of keeping time shaped by the inbreaking of a new creation.

Time tells a story. And the way we keep time inscribes that story in us. As Christians we are eighth-day people, thus the inspiration for eight-sided churches, pulpits, stained glass windows, and the emblem that adorns the cover and pages of this book. We have titled this book *Eighth Day Prayers* as an invitation to a new way of keeping time, one rooted in the rhythm of creation that nonetheless draws us on toward new creation.

In so many ways we have lost our ability to keep time. Perhaps this loss results from the movement away from an agricultural world, where land was left fallow for a season before it was sown and where sowing necessarily preceded growing, which resulted in harvest. It was impossible in the agricultural world to divorce one season from another; each season contributed its own gift and preparation to the next. But this loss of connection between the seasons is also the result of trading the church calendar for the economic calendar, where every season is harvest and none is planting.

The church calendar is not a series of discrete seasons, yet the tyranny of the economic calendar makes it initially difficult to see this. Throughout the centuries, the church has recognized that the Christian year consists of two cycles. In other words, we don't have Advent, Christmas, and Epiphany in isolation. Instead, we have the Incarnation Cycle, which consists of Advent, Christmas, and Epiphany. And we don't have Lent, Easter, and Pentecost. Instead, we have the Paschal Cycle, which consists of the three together. In each of these cycles, the seasons are intricately connected to and dependent on one another, and in each, the pattern is the same—preparation, celebration, and growth.

In a previous age, we might have simply said that mortification and repentance must precede rejoicing, because they sow the seeds for it, and that rejoicing is the foundation for growth, discipleship, and mission because we reap a harvest from the object of our rejoicing. We cannot divorce Lent from Easter, and we cannot divorce Easter from Pentecost.

Each season prepares for the next, and trying to live the spiritual life in only one season is like trying to have only harvest without sowing. We need to be planted anew each year. The Christian year offers us the framework for this.

As you let *Eighth Day Prayers* shape your daily prayers, notice how your response to Scripture and your prayers change as you contemplate what season it is. Is it a time for preparation? For rejoicing? For a rekindled awareness of God's presence and his call to us?

God himself has given us the gifts of agricultural seasons and the rhythm of the Christian year. Let that rhythm draw you more deeply into a prayer-filled life with God.

Introduction to Lent
STEVEN E. BREEDLOVE

*J*UST AS ADVENT WITHOUT CHRISTMAS MAKES NO SENSE, so Lent without Easter is meaningless. In the Christian year, celebration must follow fasting and preparation, as a seed must be sown to come to fruition. Fasting without a concluding celebration is not a Christian discipline but is instead a pagan form of self-denial.

The forty-day fast of Lent follows the biblical pattern, and in every instance—Noah, Moses, Elijah, and Jesus—a revelation from God, a blessing, or a new ministry followed the fast. The fast is intended as preparation, not an end in itself. If we seek to deny our flesh and mortify ourselves as if our own mortification is the end, then we have missed the point.

But we must also recognize that celebration in the Bible follows preparation, just as ministry follows testing and blessing follows patience. To desire Canaan without the wilderness, the Noahic covenant without forty days of rain, or the Davidic throne without exile is to miss the reality that God prepares his children for what he plans for them. If Jesus prepared for his ministry—the temptation and then Gethsemane—so also must we.

Lent, through its cycle of contrition, repentance, and self-denial, prepares the people of God to meet the risen Lord yet again. This is needed every year because the fallen world always disciples us in the wrong direction. We need a season where we realize anew our need for the cross and empty ourselves of all false hopes so that we can receive the resurrection.

Prayer during Lent is both simple and difficult. The Spirit of God invites us to confess those places where we rebel against the Lord and seek to make ourselves a god, where we still depend on our own strength. The Spirit calls us, then guides us through Scripture to examine and judge ourselves. We are called to contrition and repentance not in fear or despair but in humble honesty. The full weight of our sinfulness and the darkness of our hearts is drawn out into the open so that we are prepared to receive the life of the risen Lord yet again.

Ash Wednesday: Lent Day 1
FRANCIS CAPITANIO

Read: *Isaiah 58:6–12*

"Is not this the fast that I choose:
to loose the bonds of wickedness,
to undo the straps of the yoke,
to let the oppressed go free,
and to break every yoke?
Is it not to share your bread with the hungry
and bring the homeless poor into your house;
when you see the naked, to cover him,
and not to hide yourself from your own flesh?
Then shall your light break forth like the dawn,
and your healing shall spring up speedily;
your righteousness shall go before you;
the glory of the LORD shall be your rear guard.
Then you shall call, and the LORD will answer;
you shall cry, and he will say, 'Here I am.'
If you take away the yoke from your midst,
the pointing of the finger, and speaking wickedness,
if you pour yourself out for the hungry
and satisfy the desire of the afflicted,
then shall your light rise in the darkness
and your gloom be as the noonday.
And the LORD will guide you continually
and satisfy your desire in scorched places
and make your bones strong;
and you shall be like a watered garden,
like a spring of water,
whose waters do not fail.
And your ancient ruins shall be rebuilt;
you shall raise up the foundations of many generations;
you shall be called the repairer of the breach,
the restorer of streets to dwell in.

Reflect:

In the practice of the ancient church, fasting and almsgiving were partnered, along with works of justice. But today our selfishness often prevents us from practicing the love of God, both toward God and our neighbor. When we seek the security found in money and comfort, our success may become our prison. We may become impervious to the love and presence of God.

Isaiah declared that fasting, though important, is futile without the greater works of justice. Christ testified that his people would fast, and we know that apostles and saints have fasted up until this day. But there is also a recognition that fasting from food is a small act that trains our flesh; it is merely a reflection of the greater works we are called to do to train our hearts. These greater works teach us to see the needs of others.

Almsgiving teaches our wills to say yes to others, even as fasting trains us to say no to our stomachs. If we go through seasons of fasting but have no concern for the needs of the poor or desire to exercise our will for their sakes, then we fast in vain. We may increase in self-control regarding food, but we don't increase in self-sacrifice regarding our neighbor.

Fasting, almsgiving, and other acts of justice teach us not only what God wants in the way of self-denial but also the value of our priorities as Christians. This is why we must pray—because we can't do it alone. We must ask God to reveal who he is and what it means to follow him. As we seek to grow in him, prayer becomes the foundation on which we build our life of self-denial and contend with our flesh. This is what the season of Lent is all about.

As you pray, consider the ways you might fast during Lent, and ask the Lord to sustain you in this season.

Pray:

Lord, please train my heart and my flesh in this Lenten season. May my hunger direct my gaze heavenward so that I depend on you to be my strength. Reveal to me the needs of others so that I can be generous in your name. Amen.

Lent Day 2
SALLY BREEDLOVE

Read: *Psalm 120*

> In my distress I called to the LORD,
>   and he answered me.
> Deliver me, O LORD,
>   from lying lips,
>   from a deceitful tongue.
> What shall be given to you,
>   and what more shall be done to you,
>   you deceitful tongue?
> A warrior's sharp arrows,
>   with glowing coals of the broom tree!
> Woe to me, that I sojourn in Meshech,
>   that I dwell among the tents of Kedar!
> Too long have I had my dwelling
>   among those who hate peace.
> I am for peace,
>   but when I speak, they are for war!

Reflect:

In the first century, faithful Jews would make the ascent to Jerusalem for at least one of three major festivals celebrated each year. Jesus was raised by parents who made that annual pilgrimage, so as a boy he walked there alongside his kinfolk and neighbors.

As they traveled, he prayed and sang with them. Like every Jewish child, he was learning to pray by praying the Psalms. What was it like for the Prince of Peace to speak the words "I am for peace, but when I speak, [my words] are for war"?

When Jesus became an adult, his words stirred up controversy and hatred. While his message brought peace and life to many, in others it ignited a revulsion so strong that they planned to silence him by murder. When Jesus drew near and saw Jerusalem, he wept over it, saying, "Would that you, even you, had known on this day the things that make for peace! But now they are hidden from your eyes. . . . You did not know the time of your visitation" (Luke 19:42, 44).

We live in a time of turmoil and we can't rearrange the building blocks of our world to secure peace of mind, peace in our relationships, or peace among political parties, countries, or even peace within the scientific or religious community.

And yet we also inhabit a world where God invites us to call out to him for help each day.

As you pray, will you lament with Jesus? Will you pray for deliverance from lies, hostility, and divisive spirits both within you and around you? Will you tell the truth and admit that you need deliverance from the deception and posturing you yourself do? Will you ask Jesus to show you the things you can do in your own world to make peace?

Pray:

Eternal God, in whose perfect kingdom no sword is drawn but the sword of righteousness, no strength known but the strength of love: So mightily spread abroad your Spirit, that all peoples may be gathered under the banner of the Prince of Peace; to whom be dominion and glory now and forever. Amen.

(Anglican Church in North America Book of Common Prayer)

Lent Day 3

SALLY BREEDLOVE

Read: *Psalm 121*

> I lift up my eyes to the hills.
>> From where does my help come?
> My help comes from the LORD,
>> who made heaven and earth.
> He will not let your foot be moved;
>> he who keeps you will not slumber.
> Behold, he who keeps Israel
>> will neither slumber nor sleep.
> The LORD is your keeper;
>> the LORD is your shade on your right hand.
> The sun shall not strike you by day,
>> nor the moon by night.
> The LORD will keep you from all evil;
>> he will keep your life.
> The LORD will keep
>> your going out and your coming in
>> from this time forth and forevermore.

Reflect:

Sometimes the choice to believe is simply that—a *choice* made against despair, doubt, and fear. Can Jesus possibly understand what that tug-of-war feels like?

Imagine him as a boy. He knew the view north of Galilee with its panorama of Mount Hermon's majesty. In his trips to Jerusalem, he anticipated the hills rising to the towering temple against the southern sky. He likely sang with other pilgrims: "Does my help come from these mountains?" And he sang the response: "No, it comes from God, who created these mountains."

Christ knew the pull of doubt and the pressure to despair. Hebrews 4:15 speaks plainly about Christ's earthly experience: "For we do not have a high priest who is unable to sympathize with our weaknesses, but one who in every respect has been tempted as we are, yet without sin." The pull to disbelieve in the goodness and power of God, to want to find someone or something else to trust, is not a sin—it is a temptation.

Jesus sympathizes and wants to help us. We crave solutions to our problems, but Psalm 121—sung and prayed by pilgrims like Jesus on the road to Jerusalem—reminds us that God invites us to trust in him. In the midst of hardship, we need to be reminded again and again that we can indeed put our trust in God.

As you pray, tell your Father about your doubts, about the places in your life where it is hard to believe. Then, as Psalm 121 reminds us, say no to the doubting places in your heart. Reaffirm with Jesus and with all God's pilgrim people, "My help comes from the LORD, the Maker of heaven and earth" (Psalm 121:2 NIV).

Pray:
Lord, I believe. Help my unbelief, in Jesus's name. Amen.

Lent Day 4

SALLY BREEDLOVE

Read: *Psalm 122*

> I was glad when they said to me,
>   "Let us go to the house of the LORD!"
> Our feet have been standing
>   within your gates, O Jerusalem!
> Jerusalem—built as a city
>   that is bound firmly together,
> to which the tribes go up,
>   the tribes of the LORD,
> as was decreed for Israel,
>   to give thanks to the name of the LORD.
> There thrones for judgment were set,
>   the thrones of the house of David.
> Pray for the peace of Jerusalem!
>   "May they be secure who love you!
> Peace be within your walls
>   and security within your towers!"
> For my brothers and companions' sake
>   I will say, "Peace be within you!"
> For the sake of the house of the LORD our God,
>   I will seek your good.

Reflect:

This psalm looks toward Jerusalem; it imagines the goodness of being within the city's gates. For the Jews, Jerusalem was God's city and the temple was his dwelling place. Its walls brought safety; its unity arose from worship of the one true God. It was meant to be a place of peace—proactive peace that nurtured the well-being of all.

To travel toward Jerusalem for one of the yearly festivals was to acknowledge that the blessings we need—safety, belonging, at-oneness with others, peace, fullness of life—could not be achieved apart from worshipping God with other believing people.

As you pray, listen for the Spirit's voice. Repent of your past indifference toward gathering with other Christians. Repent of the pride that says you need to find "just the right church." Repent of your sense that you need to be a better person before you show up for worship. The psalm declares, "Our feet have been standing within your gates" (v. 2). Our dirty, travel-worn, misshapen feet—cleansed by the blood of Jesus—are welcome in God's presence.

Pray for unity. Pray for peace. Pray for leaders and pastors by name. Pray we become a people who bow in awe and love before the triune God. Pray we become a people who seek the good of all.

Pray:

Lord Jesus, you told the Samaritan woman that God seeks true worshippers. Help me to respond to your call. Shape my heart, my mind, my will, and my strength so I can live a worshipping life. Amen.

First Sunday of Lent
KARI WEST

Read: *Mark 1:16–20*

Passing alongside the Sea of Galilee, he saw Simon and Andrew the brother of Simon casting a net into the sea, for they were fishermen. And Jesus said to them, "Follow me, and I will make you become fishers of men." And immediately they left their nets and followed him. And going on a little farther, he saw James the son of Zebedee and John his brother, who were in their boat mending the nets. And immediately he called them, and they left their father Zebedee in the boat with the hired servants and followed him.

Reflect:

Jesus's ministry was just beginning at this point in Mark. His fame had yet to spread as it would just a few verses later in this chapter. What can possibly have convinced those blue-collar workers to abandon their livelihoods and follow a carpenter from the backwater of Galilee? What did their fellow fishermen think as Simon and Andrew abandoned their nets in the boat? Did Zebedee call after his sons in anger or confusion as they walked away?

"Follow me." With a single sentence, Jesus altered the course of these four men's lives. Why did they listen? Why did they trust him?

By the mysterious grace of God, they saw something true, something compelling, in Christ.

"Follow me." These words, fallen from Christ's lips and recorded for us in Scripture, have the mysterious and magnetic power as much today as they did two thousand years ago. How will you receive them today?

Will you respond in faith as Peter did: "Lord, to whom shall we go? You have the words of eternal life, and we have believed, and have come to know, that you are the Holy One of God" (John 6:68–69)? Will you follow the call of your Savior?

As you pray, allow these words to work in your soul. Dwell on the command Christ gave to all his disciples. Dwell on the beauty and truth of Jesus that compels you to obedience, even when all those around you misunderstand or scorn your steps toward the Savior. Pray for the courage you need today.

Pray:

Christ, O God, whose Son Jesus Christ is the Good Shepherd of your people: Grant that when we hear his voice, we may know him who calls us each by name, and follow where he leads; who, with you and the Holy Spirit, lives and reigns, one God, for ever and ever. Amen.

(Anglican Church in North America Book of Common Prayer)

Lent Day 5

SALLY BREEDLOVE

Read: *Psalm 123*

> To you I lift up my eyes,
>> O you who are enthroned in the heavens!
> Behold, as the eyes of servants
>> look to the hand of their master,
> as the eyes of a maidservant
>> to the hand of her mistress,
> so our eyes look to the LORD our God,
>> till he has mercy upon us.
> Have mercy upon us, O LORD, have mercy upon us,
>> for we have had more than enough of contempt.
> Our soul has had more than enough
>> of the scorn of those who are at ease,
>> of the contempt of the proud.

Reflect:

The Psalms of Ascent help us as we interact with fellow travelers and with the bystanders on the side of the road. These psalms teach us how to walk out our life together.

Are you in the midst of a hard season? What words come to mind as you finish the sentence "I have had enough of …"?

Perhaps what comes to you is best spoken only to God; it is too caustic to be said to another person. Perhaps what comes to you shames you. You ought to be a bigger person; other people have endured far worse. Can you tell the truth about your own heart? God invites us to grow in him when we tell the truth about our lives as they actually are.

This psalmist had had enough of the contempt and pride of the people around him. Perhaps he'd had enough of those who seemed to skate through life, those who didn't see themselves as pilgrims, those who had no desire or need to turn to God for help.

Listen to what he prayed as he faced a world filled with pride and contempt. He didn't pray for power to set all things right, and he didn't pray for an easier life. Instead, he reminded himself that he was God's servant. He sought God's face. He cried out to God for mercy.

We can learn from the psalmist. When the road is hard, and when people and circumstances around us make it harder, what can we do? Remember we are God's servants. Seek God's face. Cry out to him for mercy.

As you pray, name the people and situations in your life that need the mercy of God. After you name each one, simply pray, "Lord have mercy, Christ have mercy." Then pause for a moment before you mention something else. Continue to pray like this until you have held up to God the things and people that trouble you.

Pray:

To you, O Lord, we lift up our eyes. We are your servants; you are our Good Master. Have mercy, O Lord, on us and on all whom you have made; for Jesus Christ's sake. Amen.

Lent Day 6

SALLY BREEDLOVE

Read: *Psalm 124*

> If it had not been the LORD who was on our side—
> > let Israel now say—
> if it had not been the LORD who was on our side
> > when people rose up against us,
> then they would have swallowed us up alive,
> > when their anger was kindled against us;
> then the flood would have swept us away,
> > the torrent would have gone over us;
> then over us would have gone
> > the raging waters.
> Blessed be the LORD,
> > who has not given us
> > as prey to their teeth!
> We have escaped like a bird
> > from the snare of the fowlers;
> the snare is broken,
> > and we have escaped!
> Our help is in the name of the LORD,
> > who made heaven and earth.

Reflect:

Far too often, this world brings us great anguish. In the midst of suffering, we find it hard to hold to deeper truths such as the ones presented to us in Psalm 124. And yet sometimes healing comes when we join our voices with the testimony of Scripture and declare, despite our circumstances, "God is for us."

Consider the other places in Scripture that proclaim this truth:

- Romans 8:31 asks, without apology, "If God is for us, who can be against us?"
- Psalm 118:6 proclaims, "The LORD is on my side."

- When they awoke in a city surrounded by a hostile army, Elisha saw a host of angels ready to defend him, and he reassured his fearful servant, "Do not be afraid, for those who are with us are more than those who are with them" (2 Kings 6:16).

God is for us—but that does not mean he gives us a full explanation of why everything happens or why life can't be easier. God is for us—but that does not mean he is for our greed, our schemes, or our prejudices. It does not mean he is for us and, therefore, opposed to the ones we oppose.

This psalm compares the power of our enemies to the power of water: flash floods, tsunamis, dam breaks, and rising tides in hurricanes. Water—so necessary for life—in seconds is transformed into raging death. It's foolish to think we can take care of ourselves with such enemies. Still, the warrior king David rejoiced that God was for him.

The Psalms of Ascent are prayers that strengthen us to follow Jesus. They move us out of the world of our feelings and into a world defined by God's will. They're not primarily about how we feel; they're about what's true. These psalms are perfectly formed hiking boots to keep us solidly on the road for another day of walking.

As you pray, hold this truth before your own heart: "God is for me." Then hold up to God the names of those you love and those you struggle to like or forgive, and declare, "God is for _____."

Pray:

O Father God, Isaiah 43 tells us we don't have to be afraid, that we are precious in your sight and honored and loved by you. Reassure us of your love and help us to lay aside our doubts and our cynicism. Give us the humility that submits to being loved by you. Amen.

Lent Day 7

SALLY BREEDLOVE

Read: *Psalm 125*

> Those who trust in the LORD are like Mount Zion,
>   which cannot be moved, but abides forever.
> As the mountains surround Jerusalem,
>   so the LORD surrounds his people,
>   from this time forth and forevermore.
> For the scepter of wickedness shall not rest
>   on the land allotted to the righteous,
> lest the righteous stretch out
>   their hands to do wrong.
> Do good, O LORD, to those who are good,
>   and to those who are upright in their hearts!
> But those who turn aside to their crooked ways
>   the LORD will lead away with evildoers!
>   Peace be upon Israel!

Reflect:

We live in a world where the evils of racial injustice and violence often assault us. Surely God cares for the poor and marginalized who cannot protect themselves. In the times in our lives when wickedness is on full display, how can we pray a psalm that assures us that God surrounds and protects his people as he surrounds and protects Jerusalem?

Perhaps it will help to consider what Jerusalem is like. It's not a city set in an exalted location. It's a city on a hill, in the midst of a cluster of hills; no impregnable plateau keeps it safe. Jerusalem has no natural resources, no important river, and no harbor. It's not a city in a stunningly spectacular setting. Rocky hills, arid wilderness, small streams, dirt, sand, and a lake full of salt are its immediate environs. But for centuries, Jerusalem has been fought over, captured, destroyed, and rebuilt. It is a city that God has never let die as other ancient cities did.

Might the very setting of Jerusalem remind us that God loves the lowly? Might Jerusalem's history assure us that though enemy after enemy may assault the lowly, the lowly will never be utterly destroyed?

As Jesus walked to Jerusalem singing this pilgrim song, he walked toward an occupied city. What burdened his heart as he sang, "For the scepter of wickedness shall not rest on the land allotted to the righteous" (v. 3)? His earthly experience contradicted that promise, but he did not turn away in despair or turn to violence. He turned to lament. He set his face toward Jerusalem where he would lay down his life for sinners.

As you pray, lament for all that should be but is not. Lament for all that is and should not be. Ask God where you are to lay down your life for the good of others. Ask for steely-eyed endurance and a heart broken by compassion so that you will live like Jesus until God fully establishes his rule—his Jerusalem—on this earth.

Pray:

Lord, make me like your dear Son. Make me gentle and lowly of heart, courageous, quick to protect the vulnerable, patient, and faithful to endure until your kingdom comes; in the name of Jesus Christ. Amen.

Lent Day 8

MADISON PERRY

Read: *Psalm 126*

> When the LORD restored the fortunes of Zion,
>   we were like those who dream.
> Then our mouth was filled with laughter,
>   and our tongue with shouts of joy;
> then they said among the nations,
>   "The LORD has done great things for them."
> The LORD has done great things for us;
>   we are glad.
> Restore our fortunes, O LORD,
>   like streams in the Negeb!
> Those who sow in tears
>   shall reap with shouts of joy!
> He who goes out weeping,
>   bearing the seed for sowing,
> shall come home with shouts of joy,
>   bringing his sheaves with him.

Reflect:

Step outside your own circumstances and enter the world of this psalm. God's people were on a journey. They had left their homes. Rich and poor were all walking together for days, slowly ascending to the temple of the Lord.

And then, midway through, others approached the group, stragglers who looked to be from a foreign land. They hesitantly regarded one another, and then there were looks of startled recognition. Cries broke out: "Look! Our friends have returned to us!"

No one thought this was possible. Israel had been fractured, and a large portion had been carried away and forced into exile. They were never to be seen again. But here they were! They had a future now, thanks to our great God.

Return to the psalm and read it once more. Let yourself be there. Like streams in the desert, so runs the grace of our God. His salvation is known and experienced as we taste his grace together. We are exiles being welcomed home.

You may pray this psalm through tears. You have real pain—intractable injustice, the loss of work, hopeless toil against an invisible enemy, dashed hopes, private griefs, or the thwarting of all your best intentions and faithful stewardship. But God will have the final victory. For now, that moment of victory may feel like a far-off dream. But one day, your present pain will recede beyond the horizon and will linger only as a scar, a travail that the Lord carried you through.

Whom are you separated from? Who has been swept away by the awful work of sin, struck by oppression and misfortune? Pray that the Lord's grace will find these souls and bring them to a home where his justice reigns. Who has been carried away by the enemy and has forgotten their way home—who is deluded and hopeless? Pray for their forgiveness, repentance, and salvation. And in the midst of all this, pray that you will have a heart big enough to receive all exiles in love and joy. Pray that you will have the heart of Christ.

Pray:

O Lord, may your justice, grace, and peace prevail in our hearts and reign in our world. Shield us from the attacks of the evil one and grant us courage and hope. Thank you that the victory of your cross never fades and always guarantees our future. Give us real friends to help us endure until your glory comes in full. Amen.

Lent Day 9

MADISON PERRY

Read: *Psalm 127*

Unless the LORD builds the house,
    those who build it labor in vain.
Unless the LORD watches over the city,
    the watchman stays awake in vain.
It is in vain that you rise up early
    and go late to rest,
eating the bread of anxious toil;
    for he gives to his beloved sleep.
Behold, children are a heritage from the LORD,
    the fruit of the womb a reward.
Like arrows in the hand of a warrior
    are the children of one's youth.
Blessed is the man
    who fills his quiver with them!
He shall not be put to shame
    when he speaks with his enemies in the gate.

Reflect:

In vain. This phrase is repeated three times in the first two verses of today's psalm. Is there anything that can prevent our lives from being lived in vain?

Physical effort, strategic planning, careful hiring, best intentions, and emotional investment—none of these guarantee fruitfulness. Even works done *for* God suffer the same fate when they aren't done *by* God. David and Solomon, authors of our psalms, were great builders, but the works of their hands were later dashed and broken.

But notice: this psalm turns from vanity to progeny, the blessed fruit of the love of husband and wife. The fruit of our lives will be our children, including the people we have nurtured and cared for in love, prayer, and service. And the fruit of David and Solomon will not bring shame to their houses, for through their line came Jesus, son of David.

Jesus, son of David, was a master builder, though he built no citadels, temples, or palaces. He left no children behind, yet his descendants outnumber the stars in the sky. He took in strangers and made them children of God by his victory on the cross, bestowing life without end.

Jesus labors through us now, bringing life to our friends, neighbors, and enemies and reconciling all things unto himself. Even though time seems to mock us, and even though our best intentions may never add up to much, we can join in the eternally significant and sure work of building up the children of God in the name of Jesus Christ. And yes, these children will need homes, schools, churches, and statehouses. But the people with bodies and immortal souls who fill these places and grow in them will be our legacy—not the earthly monuments we leave behind.

Pray now and draw near to God's eternal temple. You are standing on a foundation that will never fade, built on the cornerstone of Christ. Jesus is expecting you, offering his blood so that you may enter this holy place. Will you allow him to welcome you and anoint you with his favor, blessing you as a child of God? Ask him for the courage to keep working even when you can't see fruit, trusting him and his will. Intercede for your parents, relatives, and friends and for this world. Ask him what you should do next.

Pray:

Father God, only you can build what lasts forever. Help me show up as your servant, day by day, in the life you have given me. Use my life to build what you desire. Grant me peace when my hard work fails; grant me faith to pour into your people; and grant me the true hope of eternal life with you and your blood-bought church; for Jesus's sake. Amen.

Lent Day 10

MADISON PERRY

Read: *Psalm 128*

> Blessed is everyone who fears the LORD,
>   who walks in his ways!
> You shall eat the fruit of the labor of your hands;
>   you shall be blessed, and it shall be well with you.
> Your wife will be like a fruitful vine
>   within your house;
> your children will be like olive shoots
>   around your table.
> Behold, thus shall the man be blessed
>   who fears the LORD.
> The LORD bless you from Zion!
>   May you see the prosperity of Jerusalem
>   all the days of your life!
> May you see your children's children!
>   Peace be upon Israel!

Reflect:

This psalm is a proclamation of blessing. The one who fears the Lord enjoys satisfying labor, family dinners, and a prosperous city. It feels so simple and idyllic—life uninterrupted by tragedy, unbroken by idolatry, and uncluttered by random commitments.

Maybe you feel that this prayer is a fantasy or a distraction. Read the psalm again. Doesn't it make you long to live in the land where God is King?

Here, then, is the best news you will hear today: Our King has come, and you can dwell in his kingdom. Jesus offered a way to eat at God's table, to have children, and to lay up treasure in a place where moth and rust do not destroy, where thieves cannot break in and steal.

Jesus had many ways of describing the kingdom. It is a reality that you may begin to know here and now, something that is growing in strength and power with the movement of the Holy Spirit.

This psalm's blessing should lead us to mourn the sin that has ravaged this world. At the same time, it calls us to begin dwelling with God in this very moment. Even now, we can receive our daily bread from the Lord. Even now, we can enjoy the slow growth of the Holy Spirit's presence. Even now, we can seek to see God's kingdom rule take hold as we respond to our circumstances with the heart of Christ.

As you pray, speak aloud your allegiance to the King of heaven and earth. Commit your own life to his rule and reign. Ask that his kingdom would come in fullness. Be specific about what will need to change in this world—and above all, in your own heart—as this happens. Praise the Lord and rest in the confidence that he who raised Jesus from the dead is at work in you.

Pray:

Almighty and everlasting God, whose will it is to restore all things in thy well-beloved Son, the King of kings and Lord of lords: Mercifully grant that the peoples of the earth, divided and enslaved by sin, may be freed and brought together under his most gracious rule; who lives and reigns with you and the Holy Spirit, one God, now and for ever. Amen.

(Anglican Church in North America Book of Common Prayer)

Second Sunday of Lent

KARI WEST

Read: *Mark 1:35–39*

> And rising very early in the morning, while it was still dark, he departed and went out to a desolate place, and there he prayed. And Simon and those who were with him searched for him, and they found him and said to him, "Everyone is looking for you." And he said to them, "Let us go on to the next towns, that I may preach there also, for that is why I came out." And he went throughout all Galilee, preaching in their synagogues and casting out demons.

Reflect:

Do you pray in the desolate places?

Other translations of these verses use the word *lonely, solitary,* or *deserted* to describe the place Christ sought early in the morning so he could speak to his Father. The word has connotations of a desert—arid, dry, and isolated.

Why did Jesus pray in such a place? Surely he did so in part for the solitude it offered him. As Simon pointed out, everyone was looking for Christ. The crowds searched for him even as Jesus searched for silence to deeply connect with his Father.

But still, why didn't Jesus seek out a beautiful and quiet setting in which to pray? Isn't there something in the loveliness and majesty of creation that draws our hearts to God? Aren't the Psalms full of effusive delight in God's handiwork that turns us to rich praise of God? Jesus knew this, and yet he chose to pray in a lonely, dry, desert-like space.

Perhaps he knew, and wanted us to know, that God will meet us in all the solitary, arid moments of our lives. It is easy to pray in an oasis; it is hard to offer petition and praise to God in a wasteland. And yet Christ rose early and sought the face of his Father in a desolate place, knowing God would meet him there. Lent is a time when we seek those desert places to be with our Father and to pour out our hearts to him.

As you pray, remember who you are in Jesus. God will always meet you in your turning toward him. Be at peace in the desolate places.

Pray:

Behold, a company of sinners at your footstool, earnestly praying to be remembered with the favor you bear unto your people, and to be visited with your salvation. We would not overlook the blessings of the life that now is. If we have food and raiment, and agreeable connections, and ease, and health, and safe abode, we would bless you; for we have no claim to these bounties, and our present condition renders them valuable. But they are not our God. . . . You are the strength of our hearts, and our portion forever. Whom have we in heaven but you; and there is none upon the earth that we desire besides you. Amen.

(William Jay)

Lent Day 11

MADISON PERRY

Read: *Psalm 129*

> "Greatly have they afflicted me from my youth"—
> > let Israel now say—
> "Greatly have they afflicted me from my youth,
> > yet they have not prevailed against me.
> The plowers plowed upon my back;
> > they made long their furrows."
> The LORD is righteous;
> > he has cut the cords of the wicked.
> May all who hate Zion
> > be put to shame and turned backward!
> Let them be like the grass on the housetops,
> > which withers before it grows up,
> with which the reaper does not fill his hand
> > nor the binder of sheaves his arms,
> nor do those who pass by say,
> > "The blessing of the LORD be upon you!
> > We bless you in the name of the LORD!"

Reflect:

As this psalm begins, the pot is boiling over. For too long the unjust have afflicted Israel. The psalm speaks with little for us to add, using images that make us recoil. "The plowers plowed upon my back; they made long their furrows" (v. 3).

It is hard to know, for at least some of us, about whom we are to pray this psalm. We don't really have enemies so much as people we wish didn't exist. But for the marginalized and discarded, the images of being furrowed strike close to home; their oppressors have faces. This psalm encourages us to identify with the least of these and to adapt their enemies as our own.

We may have complicated feelings toward someone and desire both the person's shame and salvation: "May all who hate Zion be put to shame and turned backward!" (v. 5). The curses contained in this psalm rained down on evil, seeking to wash it away. These were prayers that God's mighty Spirit would excise injustice, burn away the dross, and unflinchingly restore the glorious image that sin had almost completely obscured. In asking for justice against evildoers, the psalmist was in fact seeking their good.

The center of this psalm is the key: "The LORD is righteous" (v. 4). The pilgrims who pray this psalm don't seek vigilante justice. They turn to the Lord, trusting his hand to hold the surgical knife and his timing to do so only when it is necessary. It is the Lord who will act against the unrighteous.

We must receive this psalm within the full context of Scripture if we are to understand how to pray it. "[God] desires all people to be saved and to come to the knowledge of the truth" (1 Timothy 2:4). How does this salvation break in? Christ does not come with half-hearted blessings for the unjust and unrepentant. It is a great gift to be turned around when your every step carries you farther from God. And so, we pray for the salvation of all with the words, "Repent and believe in the gospel" (Mark 1:15).

If you don't trust yourself to pray against enemies, then simply pray the words of this psalm. If you have enemies in mind, seek their repentance, knowing that for them to repent, God must intervene with his inbreaking justice. Be aware that as you do this, you are also praying for God to operate on your own heart. Offer yourself to him and trust that he will bring his good work to completion. Ask him to bring to mind people to whom you need to apologize or steps you need to take to bring your life more completely into his kingdom reality.

Pray:
O God, we pray that your justice would reign. We pray that your will would be accomplished. We pray that saving knowledge of you would fill the earth as waters cover the sea. Come, Lord Jesus. Amen.

Lent Day 12

MADISON PERRY

Read: *Psalm 130*

> Out of the depths I cry to you, O LORD!
>> O Lord, hear my voice!
> Let your ears be attentive
>> to the voice of my pleas for mercy!
> If you, O LORD, should mark iniquities,
>> O Lord, who could stand?
> But with you there is forgiveness,
>> that you may be feared.
> I wait for the LORD, my soul waits,
>> and in his word I hope;
> my soul waits for the Lord
>> more than watchmen for the morning,
>> more than watchmen for the morning.
> O Israel, hope in the LORD!
>> For with the LORD there is steadfast love,
>> and with him is plentiful redemption.
> And he will redeem Israel
>> from all his iniquities.

Reflect:

The ascent is long, and the road has taken turns we had not anticipated. Now we enter the last, difficult, upward portion of these Psalms of Ascent at the moment before God's temple comes into view. But having walked the dusty roads and prayed the soul-searching prayers, we are plunged into the depths again.

Where do we turn when our strength is failing? We remember our Lord, and we cry out to him. We turn to him in our exhaustion. We come to him in our hunger. We flee to him for shelter from evil. We ask him for mercy. The forgiveness we know in God is the first of his blessings toward us, a firstfruit of the redemption of the whole cosmos.

In the second half of this psalm, the psalmist longed for God's redemption to be fully known. The last two stanzas are anthems to patience, the songs of someone hewn in the image of Christ who longed for daily bread and for God's kingdom.

The psalmist was aware of hunger and longing, but instead of reaching for a quick fix or instant gratification, he directed his attention to the Lord. "I wait for the LORD ... my soul waits for the Lord more than watchmen for the morning" (vv. 5–6). A night watchman is on guard at all times in case of attack, but the watchman's longing is that daylight will come without any evil occurring. A watchman waits with eager expectation, leaning toward the east and waiting for the dawn that will be visible any second now.

What depths do you call out from today? Acknowledge them and ask God for mercy. God has redeemed Israel. Ask that God's just reign would extend over the whole cosmos. God's dawn is coming, and he will not disappoint. Ask that your life will reflect the resurrection of Jesus and embolden others to hope in him. Encourage your own soul to hope in the Lord.

Pray:

Lord, you now have set your servant free
to go in peace as you have promised;
For these eyes of mine have seen the Savior,
whom you have prepared for all the world to see:
A Light to enlighten the nations,
and the glory of your people Israel.
Amen.

(The Song of Simeon)

Lent Day 13

MADISON PERRY

Read: *Psalm 131*

> O Lord, my heart is not lifted up;
>> my eyes are not raised too high;
> I do not occupy myself with things
>> too great and too marvelous for me.
> But I have calmed and quieted my soul,
>> like a weaned child with its mother;
>> like a weaned child is my soul within me.
> O Israel, hope in the Lord
>> from this time forth and forevermore.

Reflect:

After a long journey upward, at last we have passed through the gates of Jerusalem. The world outside the walls of the city fades to secondary importance. Drawn inward toward the temple, we find ourselves approaching the Holy One of Israel.

To approach the Lord in his temple, worshippers brought sacrifices that they offered to the priest. The pinnacle of all such sacrifices was humility, as Psalm 51:17 teaches: "The sacrifices of God are a broken spirit; a broken and a contrite heart, O God, you will not despise." Today's short psalm captures the essence of the sacrifice God will not despise—the humility of a worshipper of the Lord: "My heart is not lifted up" (v. 1).

The person praying it was not asking (as several of Jesus's disciples did) whether they could be the greatest in the kingdom. The psalmist did not demand to know the mysteries of the universe or God's exact plan for righting the wrongs of the world. This encounter with God was rooted in humble dependence ("my eyes are not raised too high") and led to quiet intimacy and praise.

A beautiful image captures the moment: "I have calmed and quieted my soul, like a weaned child with its mother" (v. 2). The child reclining against her mother no longer requires milk, yet she clings to her mother in joy, basking in her continued protection and nurturing.

As you pray, ask for this posture of humble joy in the presence of your Lord. Quiet your heart, refrain from clamoring for material blessings or high positions of authority, and rest securely in him. Thank God that his presence is all that we need. Ask him for the gift of hoping only in him.

Pray:

In your beauty, blessed Lord, we see a fullness of grace, truth, and righteousness. It corresponds exactly to the wants of poor sinners—your blood, to cleanse. Your grace, to comfort. Your fullness, to supply.

In you there is everything we can want: life, light, joy, pardon, mercy, peace, happiness here, glory hereafter.

Do I not see you, my King, in your beauty, when I behold you coming with all these for me? So I must cry out with the psalmist, "I love you, O Lord, my strength. The Lord is my strength and my song; And he has become my salvation." Amen.

(Robert Hawker)

Lent Day 14

MADISON PERRY

Read: *Psalm 132:7–18*

"Let us go to his dwelling place;
    let us worship at his footstool!"
Arise, O Lord, and go to your resting place,
    you and the ark of your might.
Let your priests be clothed with righteousness,
    and let your saints shout for joy.
For the sake of your servant David,
    do not turn away the face of your anointed one.
The Lord swore to David a sure oath
    from which he will not turn back:
"One of the sons of your body
    I will set on your throne.
If your sons keep my covenant
    and my testimonies that I shall teach them,
their sons also forever
    shall sit on your throne."
For the Lord has chosen Zion;
    he has desired it for his dwelling place:
"This is my resting place forever;
    here I will dwell, for I have desired it.
I will abundantly bless her provisions;
    I will satisfy her poor with bread.
Her priests I will clothe with salvation,
    and her saints will shout for joy.
There I will make a horn to sprout for David;
    I have prepared a lamp for my anointed.
His enemies I will clothe with shame,
    but on him his crown will shine."

Reflect:

This psalm captures the moment of our ascent when we enter the temple, the dwelling place of God. The Lord accepted the sacrifice of righteousness that was accomplished by Jesus Christ on the cross. We have taken on his humility. Now we dare venture in.

Praying this psalm aligns us with David as he dwelt on the significance of the temple.

And what is the centerpiece of this psalm?

More than expressing David's heart for God and for God's temple, Psalm 132 captures the Lord's heart for Zion and for the people of Zion. It reveals God's intentions for his kingdom rule on this earth. The throne of Zion is the temple, God's dwelling place among humankind.

The temple was much more than an edifice of blocks or the best place to experience song, incense, or mystical symbols. It was the focal point of God's promises and the physical manifestation of God's unshakable intention to draw our story to an end where heaven meets earth. Standing at the temple, we are overwhelmed by God's abiding love and good will toward us. We are unworthy, yet we are blessed.

Have you forgotten God's promises for you? Pray these verses aloud. God spoke them prophetically over his Son, and as you participate in Christ, they are promises for you as well. Praise him and thank him.

Pray:

Gracious God and most merciful Father, you have granted us the rich and precious jewel of your holy Word: Assist us with your Spirit, that the same Word may be written in our hearts to our everlasting comfort, to reform us, to renew us according to your own image, to build us up and edify us into the perfect dwelling place of your Christ, sanctifying and increasing in us all heavenly virtues; grant this, O heavenly Father, for Jesus Christ's sake. Amen.

(Anglican Church in North America Book of Common Prayer)

Lent Day 15

WILLA KANE

Read: *Psalm 133*

> Behold, how good and pleasant it is
> > when brothers dwell in unity!
> It is like the precious oil on the head,
> > running down on the beard,
> on the beard of Aaron,
> > running down on the collar of his robes!
> It is like the dew of Hermon,
> > which falls on the mountains of Zion!
> For there the LORD has commanded the blessing,
> > life forevermore.

Reflect:

Rarely can we use such words as *good, pleasant,* and *unified* to describe how people get along in our world. Our society, our churches, our workplaces, and our families are tragically fractured by disagreements. We are perhaps more divided today than ever before in human history.

In Psalm 133, the psalmist encouraged us to pay attention. It is both good and pleasant when people in the family get along. This psalm is a word for the people of God. Only in God is real unity possible; it is where we must begin.

But we know this isn't simple or easy. The battle between evil and good, in us and all around us, started in the garden of Eden. Broken connection with God makes unity in the human family arduous and elusive.

Can the difficulty in our lives truly work for our good and reveal God's glorious goodness? Can we find a way to truthfully say "I know the goodness of real unity with other Christians"?

Yes—but only as we draw near to God. Intimate fellowship with him is our greatest need, and his friendship makes intimate relationships with others possible. Draw near to the Father through the Son. Sense the deep love within the triune God, who is Father, Son, and Spirit. Ask God for unity of spirit with others. Ask him to teach you a deeper kind of love.

Unity is like fragrant oil anointing Aaron, the high priest, and running down his head, onto his beard, and onto his collar in excessive abundance. Oil often represents the Holy Spirit. Let God's gracious Spirit flow over and into your life; receive God's abundant provision of forgiveness, acceptance, and love.

Unity is like the dew from Mount Hermon, the highest peak, refreshing the arid climate of Mount Zion many miles away. Pause and be refreshed by the one who is living water. Experience unity, goodness, and love within the family of God.

Pray:

Father, grant us true unity with our brothers and sisters, rooted in our restored relationship with you. Please give us the love that you have for all people. Forgive us our hatred and apathy. Let us linger at the cross, freshly amazed at the lengths you went to bring us home to you. With fresh faith may we pursue friendship and love, for it is love that will mark us as your people. Amen.

Lent Day 16

WILLA KANE

Read: *Psalm 134*

> Come, bless the LORD, all you servants of the LORD,
>   who stand by night in the house of the LORD!
> Lift up your hands to the holy place
>   and bless the LORD!
> May the LORD bless you from Zion,
>   he who made heaven and earth!

Reflect:

Psalm 134 is the last of the Psalms of Ascent—those songs sung by pilgrims who journeyed from their homes in Israel to Jerusalem three times a year for festival celebrations. The Psalms of Ascent contain expressions of lament, cries for help, exclamations of confidence, and finally, shouts of praise.

This last psalm, a benediction of sorts, dwells on temple worship. But notice that the setting for this psalm is nighttime. As we walk through Lent, anticipating Easter, it is like living in the darkness, waiting for dawn, and seeking to praise God even as we wait.

Both this psalm and this season ask a question of us: How are we, as Spirit-filled servants of the Lord, to bless him when our days look as dark as night?

In this fallen world, we experience what the apostle John described: "People loved the darkness rather than the light" (John 3:19). Evil abounds on the earth; evidence that the world loves darkness is everywhere.

This psalm exhorts us, even—and especially—in the night watches, to bless the God who "is light, and in him is no darkness at all" (1 John 1:5). We are called to lift our hands to the Lord as we praise him, not only for who he is but also for what he has done for us.

We too "were darkness, but now [we] are light in the Lord" (Ephesians 5:8). Through a miracle of grace and mercy, we have joined the company of priests serving in the night watches.

Now—even if it's hard—lift your hands in praise to the Lord. Praise him that he is light. Praise him because in him there is no darkness at all.

Pray for those who are still trapped in the kingdom of darkness. Pray for real revival in Jesus. Pray the words of Isaiah from centuries ago: "The people who walked in darkness have seen a great light; those who dwelt in a land of deep darkness, on them has light shone" (Isaiah 9:2).

Pray:

Lord, in the daytime stars can be seen from deepest wells,
And the deeper the wells the brighter Thy stars shine.
Let me find Thy light in my darkness,
Thy life in my death,
Thy joys in my sorrow,
Thy grace in my sin,
Thy riches in my poverty,
Thy glory in my valley.
Amen.

(From *The Valley of Vision*)

Third Sunday of Lent

KARI WEST

Read: *Mark 3:20–34*

Then he went home, and the crowd gathered again, so that they could not even eat. And when his family heard it, they went out to seize him, for they were saying, "He is out of his mind."

And the scribes who came down from Jerusalem were saying, "He is possessed by Beelzebul," and "by the prince of demons he casts out the demons." And he called them to him and said to them in parables, "How can Satan cast out Satan? If a kingdom is divided against itself, that kingdom cannot stand. And if a house is divided against itself, that house will not be able to stand. And if Satan has risen up against himself and is divided, he cannot stand, but is coming to an end. But no one can enter a strong man's house and plunder his goods, unless he first binds the strong man. Then indeed he may plunder his house.

"Truly, I say to you, all sins will be forgiven the children of man, and whatever blasphemies they utter, but whoever blasphemes against the Holy Spirit never has forgiveness, but is guilty of an eternal sin"—for they were saying, "He has an unclean spirit."

And his mother and his brothers came, and standing outside they sent to him and called him. And a crowd was sitting around him, and they said to him, "Your mother and your brothers are outside, seeking you." And he answered them, "Who are my mother and my brothers?" And looking about at those who sat around him, he said, "Here are my mother and my brothers!"

Reflect:

The strong man was bound. Someone greater had entered the house, set on holy plundering.

This is the great truth that Christ's own family and the religious rulers missed in this passage. Christ's actions gestured toward who he was and what he would do, but those around him didn't allow themselves to see it. Instead, both his detractors and those who loved him turned to easier-to-swallow ideas. His family called him crazy, and the teachers of the law said he was possessed by the devil.

Just a few verses earlier in this chapter, unclean spirits fell before Christ and declared him to be the Son of God. And yet here, foolish leaders accused Jesus of being in league with Satan. These men were willfully blind to the great works of Jesus and what those acts revealed about his kingship and his aim. Christ rebuked them for their unbelief and arrogance.

Similarly, he told his blood family that only those who live in accordance with God's will were truly his kin. Allegiance to Jesus and belief in his lordship must supersede all earthly claims of family.

All—no matter their family status, no matter their religious knowledge or prestigious place in society—must acknowledge the lordship of Christ. He reigns over Satan, over death, over every throne and ruler and authority. He has tied up the strong man. He rules, and he will set all to rights.

As you pray, don't miss this reality as many in the passage did. Ask the Lord for fresh awareness of his dominion over all the earth and every lesser power. Pray to be an ambassador of his peace. Take refuge in him.

Pray:

Jesus, you are the image of the invisible God, the firstborn over all creation. For everything was created by you, in heaven and on earth, the visible and the invisible, whether thrones or dominions or rulers or authorities—all things have been created through you and for you. You are before all things, and by you all things hold together. Let us worship you in spirit and in truth, and in your great name. Amen.

(Adapted from Colossians 1:15–17)

Lent Day 17

MADISON PERRY

Read: *Psalm 15*

O Lord, who shall sojourn in your tent?
    Who shall dwell on your holy hill?
He who walks blamelessly and does what is right
    and speaks truth in his heart;
who does not slander with his tongue
    and does no evil to his neighbor,
    nor takes up a reproach against his friend;
in whose eyes a vile person is despised,
    but who honors those who fear the Lord;
who swears to his own hurt and does not change;
who does not put out his money at interest
    and does not take a bribe against the innocent.
He who does these things shall never be moved.

Reflect:

David began this psalm with a longing for God's home. God's tabernacle and mountain are filled with God's holiness, his resplendent glory. Home is where God's holiness dwells, and the psalmist desired to live there in unending and unsentimental fellowship with his Father.

The person who dwells with God does not find fault with those nearest him. That is, he does not judge others for their flaws and mistakes. He does not label a person according to her faults but instead allows for God's mercy and grace to prevail.

This seems to be an impossible standard—only the best and most merciful person could ever join God in his dwelling. God's home seems peaceful but inaccessible and always out of our reach. However, we have been invited to dwell in God's mountaintop home.

How? The righteous person's actions begin with truth spoken in the heart (v. 2). God wants to dwell with you, but unlike the legalistic person who judges the surface, God will begin with your heart. If you allow the Word of God to dwell within you, he will fill all of you. From the inside out, your thoughts and acts will begin to resemble those of Jesus Christ, the only truly righteous and merciful person. Once you let God through the door of your heart, he won't stop until he dwells in every square inch, preparing you for your eternal dwelling on his holy mountain.

Come to the Lord with a longing for home on his peaceful and unshakable mountain. Dwell with him now, inviting him into your thoughts, words, and deeds. Name the places where you have left off God's way and barred his entry. Thank your Father for his welcoming embrace and thank Christ for his sacrificial love. Finally, ask that God's kingdom might prevail in the world and within your own heart.

Pray:

Lord God, whose Son our Savior Jesus Christ triumphed over the powers of death and prepared for us our place in the new Jerusalem: Grant that we, who have this day given thanks for his resurrection, may praise you in that City of which he is the light, and where he lives and reigns for ever and ever. Amen.

(Anglican Church in North America Book of Common Prayer)

Lent Day 18

SALLY BREEDLOVE

Read: *Isaiah 43:1–4*

> But now thus says the LORD,
>   he who created you, O Jacob,
>   he who formed you, O Israel:
> "Fear not, for I have redeemed you;
>   I have called you by name, you are mine.
> When you pass through the waters, I will be with you;
>   and through the rivers, they shall not overwhelm you;
> when you walk through fire you shall not be burned,
>   and the flame shall not consume you.
> For I am the LORD your God,
>   the Holy One of Israel, your Savior.
> I give Egypt as your ransom,
>   Cush and Seba in exchange for you.
> Because you are precious in my eyes,
>   and honored, and I love you,
> I give men in return for you,
>   peoples in exchange for your life.

Reflect:

"Perfect love casts out fear," 1 John 4:18 promises us. What a profound mystery that love can displace fear. Most of us have known someone whose love made us feel safe. But even if we have never had that experience, our hearts long to be loved, held, and protected.

There is indeed good news that banishes fear. The triune God loves each one of us wholly. He is perfect strength and power, perfect wisdom, perfect kindness and compassion, and perfect holiness. He is the God who fully sees us—in our fears, our sin, our brokenness, and our doubt. And he is the mighty and merciful God who nonetheless fully cherishes us and protects us.

Where is your soul today? Does it feel as if the waters are rising around you? Turn to God as you pray. Be honest about where you are. Then thank him. He declares, "You are precious in my eyes, and honored, and I love you" (v. 4). Even before any feelings of being loved rise in you, thank him that he does indeed hold you in his love.

Remember that you are redeemed, called by name, and beloved by God. Even when you walk through fiery trials, he will hold you fast. You will not be consumed.

Pray:

Most loving Father, you will us to give thanks for all things, to dread nothing but the loss of you, and to cast all our care on the One who cares for us. Preserve us from faithless fears and worldly anxieties, and grant that no clouds of this mortal life may hide from us the light of that love which is immortal, and which you have manifested unto us in your Son, Jesus Christ our Lord. Amen.

(Anglican Church in North America Book of Common Prayer)

Lent Day 19

SALLY BREEDLOVE

Read: *Isaiah 50:4–10*

> Morning by morning he awakens;
>> he awakens my ear
>> to hear as those who are taught.
> The Lord GOD has opened my ear,
>> and I was not rebellious;
>> I turned not backward.
> I gave my back to those who strike,
>> and my cheeks to those who pull out the beard;
> I hid not my face
>> from disgrace and spitting.
> But the Lord GOD helps me;
>> therefore I have not been disgraced;
> therefore I have set my face like a flint,
>> and I know that I shall not be put to shame.
>> He who vindicates me is near.
> Who will contend with me?
>> Let us stand up together.
> Who is my adversary?
>> Let him come near to me.
> Behold, the Lord GOD helps me;
>> who will declare me guilty?
> Behold, all of them will wear out like a garment;
>> the moth will eat them up.
> Who among you fears the LORD
>> and obeys the voice of his servant?
> Let him who walks in darkness
>> and has no light
> trust in the name of the LORD
>> and rely on his God.

Reflect:

These words from Isaiah 50, written centuries before Jesus's birth, paint a picture of a person responsive to the Father's voice. Morning by morning, the prophet let God wake him up so he could listen and be taught.

Jesus is the fulfillment of Isaiah 50. He is the eternal God-man. As a man, he lived this listening-to-God life. He submitted to the process of learning obedience. He would not turn away or rebel. He chose to submit to injustice, disgrace, and pain. Jesus knew what it meant to suffer, to be worn out, to be mocked and mistreated, to have the light of God's presence snuffed out, and to die. That listening obedience shaped his earthly life all the way to the cross.

As you walk with Jesus, be assured that he will help you. He is not impatient with your stumbling and your doubts. He overflows with compassion. He will help you when you are weary. He will sit in the darkness with you until God brings light.

Reflect on your own life. Will you let yourself be awakened to God's Word each morning? Will you accept the hardships and injustices life brings your way? Will you choose to trust? Will you lay down your life to follow Jesus? Are you willing to wait with him in the darkness for the light that only he can bring?

Pray that God will give you the heart of a disciple, eager to listen and to obey. Ask him to calm your heart so you can wait in the darkness with Jesus. Ask him to bring peace to the fearful and weary. Ask him to make you a person of peace for others.

Pray:

Lord, we come to you because you are true life. Though we may see only death around us, when we look upon your Son, we can finally rest. Give us the energy and strength that comes from your life. Jesus bore the unimaginable weight of the sin of the world. Please give us, your feeble children, the strength to bear whatever burdens we face. Your eternal life stretches out before us undefiled by our present dangers, and we hope in you. Amen.

Lent Day 20

FRANCIS CAPITANIO

Read: *Habakkuk 3:17–19*

> Though the fig tree should not blossom,
>> nor fruit be on the vines,
> the produce of the olive fail
>> and the fields yield no food,
> the flock be cut off from the fold
>> and there be no herd in the stalls,
> yet I will rejoice in the LORD;
>> I will take joy in the God of my salvation.
> GOD, the Lord, is my strength;
>> he makes my feet like the deer's;
>> he makes me tread on my high places.

Reflect:

Add whatever it is that's not going well in your life to today's Scripture, and you will have a prayer that is always deep, always timely, and always important to hold in your heart.

There is a classic children's game called MadLibs. Players complete the blank spaces in paragraphs by adding nouns, verbs, adverbs, and adjectives of their choice; then they read their creations out loud. What they get in the end is a comical and nonsensical story that usually makes everyone laugh.

This Scripture, when filled with all our struggles, is not so funny. But what Habakkuk expresses is vital to finding the secret of contentment when we come to pray. If you add in your own worries and hardships here, what you discover in the end is a very real picture of your own need for God—not just a Savior for your sins but also a Savior for your whole life—who is able and willing to help you with whatever you may need.

This Scripture provides a prayer of true faith, a faith not based on whatever is seen around us but based on the faithfulness of God *despite* what we see around us.

As you pray, recite these words on your lips and rest in the steadfastness of God. Boldly proclaim with the psalmist, whatever your circumstances, "yet I will rejoice in the Lord; I will take joy in the God of my salvation" (v. 18). He is your strength and he will lead you to the high places. Put your trust in him.

Pray:

For all from whom God's face is hidden—by extremity of suffering, by unbelief, by loss of faith, by wickedness of men. For all righteous and faithful men, who are tempted to cast away faith or to lose confidence in God. For all who are perplexed by the darkness of divine ways, not knowing why they are afflicted. For all who are burdened and troubled for the evil and suffering permitted by God to exist. Lord, hear our prayer. Amen.

(Henry Wotherspoon)

Lent Day 21

SALLY BREEDLOVE

Read: *Jeremiah 8:18–9:1*

>My joy is gone; grief is upon me;
>>my heart is sick within me.
>Behold, the cry of the daughter of my people
>>from the length and breadth of the land:
>"Is the LORD not in Zion?
>>Is her King not in her?"
>"Why have they provoked me to anger with their carved images
>>and with their foreign idols?"
>"The harvest is past, the summer is ended,
>>and we are not saved."
>For the wound of the daughter of my people is my heart wounded;
>>I mourn, and dismay has taken hold on me.
>Is there no balm in Gilead?
>>Is there no physician there?
>Why then has the health of the daughter of my people
>>not been restored?
>Oh that my head were waters,
>>and my eyes a fountain of tears,
>that I might weep day and night
>>for the slain of the daughter of my people!

Reflect:

Are you in a season of waiting for answers or solutions that haven't come? Do you lament with Jeremiah, "We are not saved" (v. 20)?

Lent is often about waiting and sitting in darkness. With Psalm 74:10, you may find yourself crying out, "How long, O God?"

Perhaps you feel like you have been forced into a corner where there is nothing you can do to make things better. But perhaps your isolation and powerlessness is really a place of invitation. Will you learn to hope in

God, the one who is good, wise, and all powerful, even when life has gone pitch-black?

As you pray, confess your own longings and fears with a ruthless honesty. Acknowledge the places in your heart where you are wounded and admit your need for God's healing touch. Pray you will become a person who is willing to wait, to watch, and to hope.

End your prayers with the waiting words of Psalm 130.

Pray:

Out of the depths I cry to you, O Lord!
    O Lord, hear my voice!
Let your ears be attentive
    to the voice of my pleas for mercy!
If you, O Lord, should mark iniquities,
    O Lord, who could stand?
But with you there is forgiveness,
    that you may be feared.
I wait for the Lord, my soul waits,
    and in his word I hope;
my soul waits for the Lord
    more than watchmen for the morning,
    more than watchmen for the morning.
O Israel, hope in the Lord!
    For with the Lord there is steadfast love,
    and with him is plentiful redemption.
And he will redeem Israel
    from all his iniquities. Amen.

(Psalm 130)

Lent Day 22

WILLA KANE

Read: *Psalm 147:1–15*

Praise the LORD!
For it is good to sing praises to our God;
    for it is pleasant, and a song of praise is fitting.
The LORD builds up Jerusalem;
    he gathers the outcasts of Israel.
He heals the brokenhearted
    and binds up their wounds.
He determines the number of the stars;
    he gives to all of them their names.
Great is our Lord, and abundant in power;
    his understanding is beyond measure.
The LORD lifts up the humble;
    he casts the wicked to the ground.
Sing to the LORD with thanksgiving;
    make melody to our God on the lyre!
He covers the heavens with clouds;
    he prepares rain for the earth;
    he makes grass grow on the hills.
He gives to the beasts their food,
    and to the young ravens that cry.
His delight is not in the strength of the horse,
    nor his pleasure in the legs of a man,
but the LORD takes pleasure in those who fear him,
    in those who hope in his steadfast love.
Praise the LORD, O Jerusalem!
    Praise your God, O Zion!
For he strengthens the bars of your gates;
    he blesses your children within you.
He makes peace in your borders;
    he fills you with the finest of the wheat.
He sends out his command to the earth;
    his word runs swiftly.

Reflect:

The last psalms of the psalter build together into a crescendo of praise. Psalm 147 calls us four times to praise or sing thanks to the Lord. "It is good to sing praises to our God; for it is pleasant, and a song of praise is fitting" (v. 1), proclaimed the psalmist.

Amid the uncertainty of our world, is this the way you feel? Can we honestly offer praise when challenges press in on every side? We can, if we let ourselves see the ways God cares for us.

He builds up, he gathers outcasts, he heals the brokenhearted, and he binds their wounds. Our God is all-powerful. He creates, numbers, and names the stars; he covers the heavens with clouds and prepares rain for the earth. And yet God is also tender and personal. He bends low to gently lift the humble. He takes pleasure in those who fear him and trust him, who hope in his steadfast love.

Are you overwhelmed? Are you living as an outcast? Come to Jesus. Are you brokenhearted, wounded, and broken in spirit? Come to Jesus. He knows brokenness because he entered into it. He is not a stranger to the challenges you face.

He is the Word the Father sent, the Word that runs swiftly to meet your every need. Let the wind of his Spirit blow fresh life and infuse living water into your burdened heart. Experience his strength, pleasure, and peace.

The beauty of the gospel is simple, but it is not small: Put your hope in the love of God. Now rise to praise him, for he inhabits his people and takes delight in their praise. It is good to sing praises to our God.

Pray:

O Father, it is unbelievable that I, a sinner, though forgiven, am the object of your pleasure and delight. Thank you that I am among those you've gathered to yourself. I praise you with all my heart. Amen.

Fourth Sunday of Lent

KARI WEST

Read: *Mark 4:35–41*

> On that day, when evening had come, he said to them, "Let us go across to the other side." And leaving the crowd, they took him with them in the boat, just as he was. And other boats were with him. And a great windstorm arose, and the waves were breaking into the boat, so that the boat was already filling. But he was in the stern, asleep on the cushion. And they woke him and said to him, "Teacher, do you not care that we are perishing?" And he awoke and rebuked the wind and said to the sea, "Peace! Be still!" And the wind ceased, and there was a great calm. He said to them, "Why are you so afraid? Have you still no faith?" And they were filled with great fear and said to one another, "Who then is this, that even the wind and the sea obey him?"

Reflect:

"Do you not care that we are perishing?" (v. 38).

Christ responded to his disciples' question with a display of his absolute power over the creation he had made. Then he turned and asked his disciples, "Why are you afraid? After all this time, do you still not know who I am? Is your faith still so weak?"

Christ replaced their fear with a better one. Instead of towering waves, swift winds, or the threat of death, he himself was put on display as the one to hold in awe as the Supreme Ruler of the earth. But Christ was very different from earthly rulers. He used his power to protect, to heal, and to bring peace. He directed his might to harness chaos and to still the storm.

The disciples feared death and distrusted Jesus. But Christ knew, with the long path ahead of them—which would end for most in their martyrdoms— that they needed a radical reorientation of their fears. He displayed his power so that when the time came for the disciples to face death, they would trust their resurrected and risen Savior, creation's Lord and death's trampler.

As you pray, remember that Lent is all about following Christ in this long walk of obedience and faith. Thank Christ for his power, his care, and his love. Hope in him as death's foe, as the earth's ruler, and as your ever-near friend. Ask him again for the steadfastness to follow where he leads.

Pray:

Grant, Almighty God, that as you see us laboring under so much weakness, yes, with our minds so blinded that our faith falters at the smallest perplexities, and almost fails altogether—O grant that by the power of your Spirit we may be raised up above this world, and learn more and more to renounce our own counsels, and so come to you, that we may stand fixed in our watchtower, ever hoping through your power for whatever you have promised us, though you should not immediately make it manifest to us that you have faithfully spoken. Amen.

(John Calvin)

Lent Day 23

KARI WEST

Read: *Psalm 51:1–12*

> Have mercy on me, O God,
>> according to your steadfast love;
> according to your abundant mercy
>> blot out my transgressions.
> Wash me thoroughly from my iniquity,
>> and cleanse me from my sin!
> For I know my transgressions,
>> and my sin is ever before me.
> Against you, you only, have I sinned
>> and done what is evil in your sight,
> so that you may be justified in your words
>> and blameless in your judgment.
> Behold, I was brought forth in iniquity,
>> and in sin did my mother conceive me.
> Behold, you delight in truth in the inward being,
>> and you teach me wisdom in the secret heart.
> Purge me with hyssop, and I shall be clean;
>> wash me, and I shall be whiter than snow.
> Let me hear joy and gladness;
>> let the bones that you have broken rejoice.
> Hide your face from my sins,
>> and blot out all my iniquities.
> Create in me a clean heart, O God,
>> and renew a right spirit within me.
> Cast me not away from your presence,
>> and take not your Holy Spirit from me.
> Restore to me the joy of your salvation,
>> and uphold me with a willing spirit.

Reflect:

When sin is revealed in your life, is your first reaction to hide it, justify it, or minimize it? Or do you take it to God in prayer? How often do you confess your failures to the Lord?

The arrogant are blind to their own iniquity, but a person who seeks to walk in humility and live with a right understanding of his or her own soul before God will discover how much sin still lurks within. It takes a humble heart and great courage to acknowledge and confess that sin.

But the beautiful reality is that the more we make a habit of confession and repentance, the more we will grasp God's deep capacity to cleanse us from sin, to pull us farther into sanctification, and to purify our hearts and minds. God is the one who gives clean hearts, who renews right spirits, who restores and upholds. All we must do is continually ask for humility, grace, and the courage to confess and repent. God promises to blot out our transgressions, to wash us thoroughly, and to save us to the uttermost.

Take time to sit in silence before the Lord, asking him to reveal any sins that you need to confess. Allow the Holy Spirit to do his convicting work in your soul. Confess, repent, and receive God's mercy and grace to walk in a way that honors him. Be at peace.

Pray:

O Lord, open my lips,
    and my mouth will declare your praise.
For you will not delight in sacrifice, or I would give it;
    you will not be pleased with a burnt offering.
The sacrifices of God are a broken spirit;
    a broken and contrite heart, O God, you will not despise. Amen.

(Psalm 51:15–17)

Lent Day 24

KARI WEST

Read: *Psalm 109:1–5, 21–31*

Be not silent, O God of my praise!
For wicked and deceitful mouths are opened against me,
   speaking against me with lying tongues.
They encircle me with words of hate,
   and attack me without cause.
In return for my love they accuse me,
   but I give myself to prayer.
So they reward me evil for good,
   and hatred for my love....
But you, O GOD my Lord,
   deal on my behalf for your name's sake;
   because your steadfast love is good, deliver me!
For I am poor and needy,
   and my heart is stricken within me.
I am gone like a shadow at evening;
   I am shaken off like a locust.
My knees are weak through fasting;
   my body has become gaunt, with no fat.
I am an object of scorn to my accusers;
   when they see me, they wag their heads.
Help me, O LORD my God!
   Save me according to your steadfast love!
Let them know that this is your hand;
   you, O LORD, have done it!
Let them curse, but you will bless!
   They arise and are put to shame, but your servant will be glad!
May my accusers be clothed with dishonor;
   may they be wrapped in their own shame as in a cloak!
With my mouth I will give great thanks to the LORD;
   I will praise him in the midst of the throng.
For he stands at the right hand of the needy one,
   to save him from those who condemn his soul to death.

68

Reflect:

In Psalm 109, the goodness and steadfastness of our ruling God starkly was contrasted with the evil, lying leaders who oppressed David. These men were so aligned with a life of wickedness that David said they wore cursing like a garment and displayed their shame as their outer cloak. Because of their malice, David felt he was fading away like a shadow in the evening. He felt as insignificant as an insect.

But in the midst of these deep difficulties, David sought the face of God. He called on the Lord to act according to his character and his faithful love. Although these leaders cursed, David called on God to bless. Although these leaders oppressed the poor and trod over the lowly, David named God as the one who stands at the right hand of the needy.

Rather than give in to despair because of these men's brutality and power, David recalled the supremacy of God. He pleaded with the Lord of heaven and earth to bring justice against those who maligned and abused his people. He rested in the surety that he would praise God in a throng of worshippers. God will sit enthroned forever, long after all evil rulers are put to shame. His justice will shine like the noonday sun.

As you pray, take heart in God's reigning power. Lent is a time of sorrow and of repentance, but it is never a time of despair. Ask God to bring justice and deliverance to this world. Hope in his eternal throne.

Pray:

With my mouth I will greatly extol you, Lord; in the great throng of worshippers, I will praise you. For you stand at the right hand of the needy, to save their lives from those who would condemn them. Amen.

(Adapted from Psalm 109)

Lent Day 25
WILLA KANE

Read: *Luke 18:35–43*

> As he drew near to Jericho, a blind man was sitting by the roadside begging. And hearing a crowd going by, he inquired what this meant. They told him, "Jesus of Nazareth is passing by." And he cried out, "Jesus, Son of David, have mercy on me!" And those who were in front rebuked him, telling him to be silent. But he cried out all the more, "Son of David, have mercy on me!" And Jesus stopped and commanded him to be brought to him. And when he came near, he asked him, "What do you want me to do for you?" He said, "Lord, let me recover my sight." And Jesus said to him, "Recover your sight; your faith has made you well." And immediately he recovered his sight and followed him, glorifying God. And all the people, when they saw it, gave praise to God.

Reflect:

Jesus was making his way through Jericho to Jerusalem and to the cross. He had just described in detail what lay ahead, but his closest friends were blind to his teaching.

Yet even though he was headed to the cross, Christ's heart was still full of compassion. For three years, Jesus had blessed people with countless miracles, beginning in northern Israel at a wedding in Galilee. Now this last miracle before his resurrection took place on his journey to Jerusalem.

As he traveled, Jesus was surrounded by loud throngs of pilgrims who were also on their way to celebrate Passover in Jerusalem. From the crowd, a beggar cried out, "Jesus, Son of David" (v. 38). The crowd tried to hush him, but he persisted. The very fact that he called Jesus "Son of David" would have startled the crowd. What made this man think that Jesus was the promised Messiah? "Have mercy on me!" (v. 39), he cried out again.

Jesus called for the blind man to come to him. The blind beggar came, he believed, and his dead eyes were transformed by the power of Christ.

Mark's account adds an important detail: Unlike the rich young ruler who chose possessions over Jesus, this man threw away the only thing he had, a worn-out cloak, and ran to Christ (Mark 10).

Jesus asked him a simple question: "What do you want me to do for you?" His answer: "Lord, I want to see" (v. 41 NIV). As the crowd looked on, faith became sight. Seeing, the man followed his Savior.

Take a moment to consider Jesus. The one he blessed in this story was a blind beggar, an outcast at the bottom of society, rejected by family and dependent on charity from strangers. Paradoxically, in his blindness, the beggar saw more than the disciples who had been with Jesus for three years. He saw with the eyes of his heart.

As you pray, ask Jesus to open the eyes of your heart. Thank him for the miracle of new life in him, and ask for renewed purpose to follow him well, not just during Lent but for all the days of your life.

Pray:

Lord, high and holy, meek and lowly,
You have brought me to the valley of vision,
where I live in the depths but see You in the heights;
hemmed in by mountains of sin I behold your glory.
Let me learn by paradox that the way down is the way up,
that to be low is to be high,
that the broken heart is the healed heart,
that the contrite spirit is the rejoicing spirit,
that the repenting soul is the victorious soul,
that to have nothing is to possess all,
that to bear the cross is to wear the crown,
that to give is to receive,
that the valley is the place of vision. Amen.

(From *The Valley of Vision*)

Lent Day 26

SALLY BREEDLOVE

Read: *Mark 5:21–24, 35–42*

And when Jesus had crossed again in the boat to the other side, a great crowd gathered about him, and he was beside the sea. Then came one of the rulers of the synagogue, Jairus by name, and seeing him, he fell at his feet and implored him earnestly, saying, "My little daughter is at the point of death. Come and lay your hands on her, so that she may be made well and live." And he went with him....

While he was still speaking, there came from the ruler's house some who said, "Your daughter is dead. Why trouble the Teacher any further?" But overhearing what they said, Jesus said to the ruler of the synagogue, "Do not fear, only believe." And he allowed no one to follow him except Peter and James and John the brother of James. They came to the house of the ruler of the synagogue, and Jesus saw a commotion, people weeping and wailing loudly. And when he had entered, he said to them, "Why are you making a commotion and weeping? The child is not dead but sleeping." And they laughed at him. But he put them all outside and took the child's father and mother and those who were with him and went in where the child was. Taking her by the hand he said to her, "Talitha cumi," which means, "Little girl, I say to you, arise." And immediately the girl got up and began walking (for she was twelve years of age), and they were immediately overcome with amazement.

Reflect:

People who have succeeded in life often have a hard time accepting help. Jairus had arrived. He was the ruler of the synagogue in his region. He was known; he was important. Jesus was the controversial young itinerant rabbi who was welcomed by some and run out of town by others.

But Jairus was desperate. His beloved twelve-year-old daughter was dying. He would risk his reputation and do anything to save her, even if it meant asking Jesus for help. Humbling himself, Jairus didn't send a messenger but instead went and fell at Jesus's feet.

Wonderfully, Jesus began to follow Jairus to his house, but then Jairus faced another opportunity for humility. Jesus stopped in his tracks to help a nobody woman. She was not the adolescent daughter of a well-to-do man. She was middle-aged, unclean, hopeless, and without family. But she, too, was determined to seek Jesus's help.

Despite the protests of his disciples, Christ stopped to care for this woman. Desperate fear and anger likely rose up in Jairus. They could not delay! His daughter was dying.

The worst happened. Although the woman was healed, messengers arrived from Jairus's household with a soul-killing message: His daughter was dead. Pause and let Jairus's despair touch you. Was he overcome with his loss? Was he angry at the woman and at Jesus's delay? Were his thoughts flashing ahead to his wife's anguish and the emptiness that would haunt their home? Did he have a stab of fear that he had forfeited his status by turning to Jesus?

Before Jairus could respond, Jesus spoke. The verbs Mark used in this passage are best translated "Don't go on fearing the worst. Keep on believing the best."

Pause now as you prepare to pray. Lent is a time to learn humility. Are you willing to humble yourself and ask Jesus to help you? Are you willing to humble yourself and accept the hope he offers? Don't go on fearing the worst; keep on believing the best. Pray for the grace to run to Jesus, to wait for Jesus, and to know that Jesus is stronger than death itself.

Pray:

Lord, all of us grieve someone who has died. O help us in the depth of our loss and pain. Help us to trust that you will make all things new. Lord, all of us find stubborn places in our hearts where we don't want to ask you for help. Forgive our anger, our impatience, our sense of entitlement, and our despair. Teach us to keep on believing; for Jesus's sake. Amen.

Lent Day 27

SALLY BREEDLOVE

Read: *Mark 6:1–6*

> He went away from there and came to his hometown, and his
> disciples followed him. And on the Sabbath he began to teach in
> the synagogue, and many who heard him were astonished, saying,
> "Where did this man get these things? What is the wisdom given to
> him? How are such mighty works done by his hands? Is not this the
> carpenter, the son of Mary and brother of James and Joses and Judas
> and Simon? And are not his sisters here with us?" And they took
> offense at him. And Jesus said to them, "A prophet is not without
> honor, except in his hometown and among his relatives and in his
> own household." And he could do no mighty work there, except
> that he laid his hands on a few sick people and healed them. And he
> marveled because of their unbelief.
>
> And he went about among the villages teaching.

Reflect:

Mark took pains to show us that many people rejected Jesus: the skeptical
scribes as he offered forgiveness and healing to a paralyzed man, John's disciples and the Pharisees who questioned if Jesus was truly righteous, and both
the Pharisees and the politically powerful Herodians in their murderous
opposition. After Jesus's Sabbath miracles, unclean spirits tried to expose
him, his extended family doubted his sanity, the scribes accused him of being
demon-possessed, his disciples complained that he didn't really care about
them, and the Gerasenes banished him from their town.

This rejection continued in Mark 6. Jesus had gone home to Nazareth.
He was no longer a carpenter. His band of disciples and his teaching marked
him as a rabbi, and the miracles he had done suggested he was far more than
a rabbi. Surely in Nazareth he would be welcomed?

After all, the people in Nazareth were his kinfolk and neighbors. They had bargained and traded with Jesus for him to build them a table, a house, or a new yoke. Jesus had been a workman like the rest of them.

They knew his character. He had never been false, never used anyone, never pawned off shoddy workmanship, and never erupted in anger, drunkenness, or greed. Even as a boy, he was the only truly good person.

How could they not believe? But Mark was clear. Their astonishment that their local boy was no longer simply a carpenter turned to contempt and resistance. They didn't want to listen, to believe, or to receive Jesus's help.

As you pray, thank Jesus for enduring your own hostility toward him. Thank him for being patient with your doubt and for forgiving your contempt. Ask Christ to give you a child's welcoming heart, one eager to believe him, trust him, and follow him.

Pray:

Almighty God, give us the increase of faith, hope, and love; and, that we may obtain what you have promised, make us love what you command; through Jesus Christ our Lord, who lives and reigns with you and the Holy Spirit, one God, for ever and ever. Amen.

(Anglican Church in North America Book of Common Prayer)

Lent Day 28

SALLY BREEDLOVE

Read: *Mark 6:45–52*

Immediately he made his disciples get into the boat and go before him to the other side, to Bethsaida, while he dismissed the crowd. And after he had taken leave of them, he went up on the mountain to pray. And when evening came, the boat was out on the sea, and he was alone on the land. And he saw that they were making headway painfully, for the wind was against them. And about the fourth watch of the night he came to them, walking on the sea. He meant to pass by them, but when they saw him walking on the sea they thought it was a ghost, and cried out, for they all saw him and were terrified. But immediately he spoke to them and said, "Take heart; it is I. Do not be afraid." And he got into the boat with them, and the wind ceased. And they were utterly astounded, for they did not understand about the loaves, but their hearts were hardened.

Reflect:

After feeding the five thousand, Christ made his disciples get in a boat and begin the journey across the Sea of Galilee. Perhaps, as John hinted in his version, Jesus knew that his disciples might be caught up in the movement by the crowd to make him king. Maybe he was protecting them from short-sighted foolishness. Jesus dismissed the crowd (and his disciples) and climbed a mountain to pray. Finally, he had time to be with his Father. He lingered there.

As the night unfolded, Jesus looked toward the water. It was whipped into a fever pitch by a windstorm. Perhaps the moon was full; perhaps dawn was emerging. Jesus saw his friends straining to cross the lake. He walked down to the shoreline and began to walk on the rough sea. We assume he would join his friends in the boat and help them. We assume he would quiet the sea.

Mark's gospel surprises us: "He meant to pass by them" (v. 48). "Why?" we ask. For their part, the disciples were frightened. Thinking that Jesus was a ghost, they cried out in fear. Where was their faith? Could they not reason that the one who had fed five thousand would also be able to walk on water or calm a storm?

This simple story raises questions we can't answer. We'll never understand everything Jesus does. We become afraid in overwhelming circumstances. Often, we don't even hold on to the faith we were given the last time we went through a similar crisis. What do we do?

Perhaps the best thing is simply to return to the words of Christ. "Take heart; it is I. Do not be afraid" (v. 50). We can hold these words when we are deeply confused and scared. Christ is near, and he is with us. His reality is greater than any confusion and every storm. We will never be abandoned.

As you pray, thank Jesus that he is always present and always able to help you. Submit by faith to what you do not understand. Ask him to strengthen your believing.

Pray:

May that good Spirit of Jesus Christ open the eyes of our minds, that we may see and approve things that are excellent. May he persuade our hearts to receive that truth in the love of it, and direct our steps to walk in the paths of mercy and truth, that we may be saved. Amen.

(William Ames)

Fifth Sunday of Lent

MADISON PERRY

Read: *Mark 7:14–23*

> And he called the people to him again and said to them, "Hear me, all of you, and understand: There is nothing outside a person that by going into him can defile him, but the things that come out of a person are what defile him." And when he had entered the house and left the people, his disciples asked him about the parable. And he said to them, "Then are you also without understanding? Do you not see that whatever goes into a person from outside cannot defile him, since it enters not his heart but his stomach, and is expelled?" (Thus he declared all foods clean.) And he said, "What comes out of a person is what defiles him. For from within, out of the heart of man, come evil thoughts, sexual immorality, theft, murder, adultery, coveting, wickedness, deceit, sensuality, envy, slander, pride, foolishness. All these evil things come from within, and they defile a person."

Reflect:

This passage reveals to us Jesus's overwhelming concern for us and his desire to protect us from ourselves.

In Jesus's time, religious people struggled under the weight of a ubiquitous worry that they had to protect themselves from the negative influence of the world around them. They believed that if they could isolate themselves from outside trouble and corrupting objects and people, they would finally be holy.

This same instinct is still with us today. If only we could be left alone and spared the awful influence of any number of morally repugnant outsiders, then we could live lives that would be pleasing to God.

But Jesus changed the conversation and put the focus on our hearts. "There is nothing outside a person that by going into him can defile him, but the things that come out of a person are what defile him. . . . For from within, out of the heart of man, come evil thoughts" (vv. 15, 21).

We have sold our very hearts for a mess of pottage—cheap thrills, easy pleasure, gratifying anger—and now we are in bondage. Our instinct is to lose track of our moral failings by fretting constantly over the evils being played out on the world stage or in our neighbor's living room. Jesus put the focus back on us.

As we turn to the Lord in prayer, let us remember that God is real, unchanging, and ever-present, regardless of whatever we fear is at work in the world. Jesus, our Creator and Author, knows more of the human heart than we ever will.

Take another look at the evil things that Jesus says come from within. Pray that God will renew your heart. Return to the joy of the salvation wrought in Christ!

Pray:

O God, the King eternal, whose light divides the day from the night and turns the shadow of death into the morning: Drive far from us all wrong desires, incline our hearts to keep your law, and guide our feet into the way of peace; that, having done your will with cheerfulness during the day, we may, when night comes, rejoice to give you thanks; through Jesus Christ our Lord. Amen.

(Anglican Church in North America Book of Common Prayer)

Lent Day 29

MADISON PERRY

Read: *Mark 7:31–37*

Then he returned from the region of Tyre and went through Sidon to the Sea of Galilee, in the region of the Decapolis. And they brought to him a man who was deaf and had a speech impediment, and they begged him to lay his hand on him. And taking him aside from the crowd privately, he put his fingers into his ears, and after spitting touched his tongue. And looking up to heaven, he sighed and said to him, "Ephphatha," that is, "Be opened." And his ears were opened, his tongue was released, and he spoke plainly. And Jesus charged them to tell no one. But the more he charged them, the more zealously they proclaimed it. And they were astonished beyond measure, saying, "He has done all things well. He even makes the deaf hear and the mute speak."

Reflect:

We read here an astonishingly intimate scene. Jesus drew a deaf man aside from the crowd, privately working a miracle for one who could never do anything for him in return: "And taking him aside from the crowd privately, he put his fingers into his ears, and after spitting touched his tongue" (v. 33).

Putting fingers in ears, spitting, and touching his tongue—these are the kinds of actions parents perform for their children. But here we see Jesus, the Author of life, perform an act of re-creation on behalf of a beloved child.

This scene overflows with weakness and tenderness. We feel embarrassed to look. But we mustn't turn away. Let this pitiful person who lacked ears to hear, or even a tongue to speak, show us what we need to understand. We too are children, unable to help ourselves. We are children who must admit our vulnerability and confess our need for the tender care of our Father.

As you approach the Lord, consider his offer of salvation for you and for those you know. Call to mind your own weakness. Allow Jesus to see you for who you are; allow him to do what he must. Do not shy away from his intimate, restorative touch. Even if he must put his fingers in your ears and touch your tongue with his spit, rejoice that the one who made you has recreated you. Rest in his care.

Pray:

Late have I loved you,
O Beauty so ancient and so new,
late have I loved you!
Lo, you were within,
but I outside, seeking there for you,
and upon the shapely things you have made
I rushed headlong—I, misshapen.
You were with me, but I was not with you.
They held me back far from you,
those things which would have no being,
were they not in you.
You called, shouted, broke through my deafness;
you flared, blazed, banished my blindness;
you lavished your fragrance, I gasped; and now I pant for you;
I tasted you, and now I hunger and thirst;
you touched me, and I burned for your peace.
Amen.

(Augustine of Hippo)

Lent Day 30

MADISON PERRY

Read: *Mark 8:27–30*

> And Jesus went on with his disciples to the villages of Caesarea Philippi. And on the way he asked his disciples, "Who do people say that I am?" And they told him, "John the Baptist; and others say, Elijah; and others, one of the prophets." And he asked them, "But who do you say that I am?" Peter answered him, "You are the Christ." And he strictly charged them to tell no one about him.

Reflect:

What brings you back to the Lord today? Routine and rhythm? The need to make someone else happy? The hope of receiving healing or blessing?

At this moment in Mark 8, Jesus was turning toward the cross. He had revealed his immense power and his all-encompassing heart for others. He had begun to fend off a host of expectations placed on him by religious and political authorities. He had set his face to deal the decisive blow against sin and evil. The stakes couldn't be higher, but so few had even begun to grasp who he was. Even among those who walked with Jesus, there was confusion over his identity. Was he a prophet? Elijah? John the Baptist?

This scene invites us to stand alongside Jesus's disciples. The one we sometimes make into a plaything or a dispenser of blessing stands before us. His love encompasses the whole world and descends into the deepest depths of our souls. Jesus came to set his creation free, to set *you* free. He wants you to see him for who he is and proclaim him in thought, word, and deed all the days of your life.

Jesus's question is meant to probe the depths of our hearts. Listen as he asks, "But who do you say that I am?" (v. 29).

Search yourself and answer in prayer. Embrace Jesus as Savior. Disregard the competing voices in your world that would make little of Jesus. Ask Jesus himself for a strong faith and solid convictions. Pray for the courage to follow him wherever he leads. Lift your voice to the Lord in praise of who he is. Praise him for the works of his hand and thank him for his invitation to you today.

Pray:

You called for my heart.

Oh that it were in any way fit for your acceptance!

I am unworthy, Lord, everlastingly unworthy to be yours.

But since you will have it so, I freely give my heart to you.

Take it; it is yours.

Oh that it were better!

But Lord, I put it into your hand, who alone can mend it.

Mold it after your own heart.

Make it as you would have it—humble, heavenly, soft, tender, and flexible.

Write your law on it.

Amen.

(Joseph Alleine)

Lent Day 31

SALLY BREEDLOVE

Read: *Mark 8:31, 34–37*

And he began to teach them that the Son of Man must suffer many
things and be rejected by the elders and the chief priests and the
scribes and be killed, and after three days rise again....

And calling the crowd to him with his disciples, he said to them,
"If anyone would come after me, let him deny himself and take up
his cross and follow me. For whoever would save his life will lose
it, but whoever loses his life for my sake and the gospel's will save it.
For what does it profit a man to gain the whole world and forfeit his
soul? For what can a man give in return for his soul?"

Reflect:

How did we ever get it into our heads that the journey to the life we really
want would be easy?

The universe reminds us that life is born out of death. There is a rhythmic
dying hidden in each season: the loss of the safety of the womb through the
risk of birth, the laying down of one's independence and autonomy for the
good union of marriage, the seeds that die for vegetables and flowers to grow,
and the peach blossoms that wither and fall to the ground so bubbly hot
peach crisp can crown a summer supper. Death is the door to life.

It's almost Easter, the yearly celebration of the Lord Jesus Christ's death
and resurrection. The resurrection is God's lived-out-in-history proclamation
that life is stronger than death, and it is the reminder that in God's mystery,
life must pass through death if it is to offer life to others. A Jesus who never
died would be only a paragon of virtue, not the Son of God whose death
gives life. The death of Jesus destroyed death itself and opened the door to
new life.

What has been dying in you lately? God promises to bring real life out of
what dies. As you pray, can you hold up what you love, what you count on,
and what gives you joy as offerings to God? Pray that the deaths you die may

bring life to others. Pray that God will give you a heart and vision for the kind of dying that can bring life to others.

Ask God to show you something life-giving you can do for someone who is hurting or alone. As you pray, call to mind someone whose losses and griefs are far greater than your own. Pray that over time, the Holy Spirit will help this person see life emerge from the death he or she is experiencing.

Pray:

Father, there is death at work in us, pulling us toward despair. Our attempts to comfort ourselves and to ignore our condition have not worked, so we lay down our lives before you now, acknowledging you as Master and Lord. Purge sin and death from us, both in the depths of our souls and in our daily decisions. Keep us from living to make ourselves happy. We embrace the true life that comes to us through the death and resurrection of Jesus Christ. In ways large and small, may we die to ourselves and know your immovable peace and energizing joy. May you be glorified in our lives; in the name of the Father, Son, and Holy Spirit. Amen.

Lent Day 32

BRANDON WALSH

Read: *Mark 12:13–17*

And they sent to him some of the Pharisees and some of the
Herodians, to trap him in his talk. And they came and said to him,
"Teacher, we know that you are true and do not care about anyone's
opinion. For you are not swayed by appearances, but truly teach the
way of God. Is it lawful to pay taxes to Caesar, or not? Should we
pay them, or should we not?" But, knowing their hypocrisy, he said
to them, "Why put me to the test? Bring a denarius and let me
look at it." And they brought one. And he said to them, "Whose
likeness and inscription is this?" They said to him, "Caesar's." Jesus
said to them, "Render to Caesar the things that are Caesar's, and to
God the things that are God's." And they marveled at him.

Reflect:

Religious leaders who were trying to trap Jesus asked him a hot political
question: "Is it lawful to pay taxes to Caesar?" (v. 14). Jesus's answer offers us
a framework for thinking about our own politics.

Jesus asked them to bring a coin to him. Then he looked at it and asked,
"Whose likeness and inscription is this?" They all replied, "Caesar's." Jesus
responded, "Render to Caesar the things that are Caesar's, and to God the
things that are God's" (vv. 16–17).

To modern readers, this statement can be perplexing. We are supposed
to pay taxes because of the picture on the coin? What was Jesus driving at?
What does it mean to us now?

In Exodus 20:4, Moses presented the Ten Commandments to the
Israelites, the second of them being, "You shall not make for yourself a carved
image, or any likeness of anything that is in heaven above, or that is in the
earth beneath, or that is in the water under the earth." This commandment
instructed God's people to refrain from worshipping anything other than the
Lord and to refrain from creating images on objects of worship. The deep

logic was that in the temple of creation, human beings are the ones who bear the image of God.

When Jesus took the coin graven with the image of Caesar, he made the profound point that if Caesar wanted some of his silver, then we should give it to him; but we are made in the image of God, and we belong to him.

The same is true today. As Christians, we live in a society and should "give unto Caesar," meaning we should be faithful to fulfill our civil obligations, pay taxes, and work toward the common good. But we must never confuse the image on the coin for the image written into us. Our deepest, fullest, and most primary identity must be found in the living image of the invisible God, Jesus Christ (Colossians 1:15). Some trust in chariots and horses, but our ultimate hope always rests on the kingdom of God rather than any temporal poltical reality.

We have something greater to love than images on coins or the people whom they represent. Take heart: We have a true and living God. As you pray, remember that he whom you worship is greater than he who is in the world. Thank God for his supremacy and ask for greater faith to trust in him.

Pray:

Almighty God, our heavenly Father, send down on those who hold public office, especially those just elected, the spirit of wisdom, charity, and justice; that with steadfast purpose they may faithfully serve in their offices to promote the well-being of all people; through Jesus Christ our Lord. Amen.

(Anglican Church in North America Book of Common Prayer)

Lent Day 33
BRANDON WALSH

Read: *Mark 12:38–44*

> And in his teaching he said, "Beware of the scribes, who like to walk around in long robes and like greetings in the marketplaces and have the best seats in the synagogues and the places of honor at feasts, who devour widows' houses and for a pretense make long prayers. They will receive the greater condemnation."
>
> And he sat down opposite the treasury and watched the people putting money into the offering box. Many rich people put in large sums. And a poor widow came and put in two small copper coins, which make a penny. And he called his disciples to him and said to them, "Truly, I say to you, this poor widow has put in more than all those who are contributing to the offering box. For they all contributed out of their abundance, but she out of her poverty has put in everything she had, all she had to live on."

Reflect:

Jesus's words offer insight into the nature of worship and giving. Jesus compared wealthy people making big donations, their coins loudly clanging into the temple coffers, with a humble widow quietly offering her two coins. The first group offered a huge amount of money but did not offer themselves to God; instead, they offered themselves up for the praise of others. The widow, on the other hand, gave out of her poverty. She gave herself.

The resources we offer to the Lord are symbols of our whole lives, offered up to the Lord as an ongoing act of worship. The Lord wants your pocketbook, but not because he needs the money!

The Lord owns the cattle on a thousand hills. The Lord desires our offerings because they represent all that we are and all that we have. The actual amount of money, time, and talents we offer the Lord may change depending on our circumstances—but we are all called to offer ourselves wholeheartedly.

As you pray, ask the Lord for an increased heart of generosity. Ask to grow in true worship in offering your whole life to him. Thank him for his provision and his love.

Pray:

Grant, O God, that we may follow the example of your faithful servant Barnabas, who, seeking not his own renown but the well-being of your Church, gave generously of his life and substance for the relief of the poor, and went forth courageously in mission for the spread of the Gospel; through Jesus Christ our Lord, who lives and reigns with you and the Holy Spirit, one God, for ever and ever. Amen.

(Anglican Church in North America Book of Common Prayer)

Lent Day 34

BRANDON WALSH

Read: *Mark 13:28–37*

"From the fig tree learn its lesson: as soon as its branch becomes tender and puts out its leaves, you know that summer is near. So also, when you see these things taking place, you know that he is near, at the very gates. Truly, I say to you, this generation will not pass away until all these things take place. Heaven and earth will pass away, but my words will not pass away.

"But concerning that day or that hour, no one knows, not even the angels in heaven, nor the Son, but only the Father. Be on guard, keep awake. For you do not know when the time will come. It is like a man going on a journey, when he leaves home and puts his servants in charge, each with his work, and commands the doorkeeper to stay awake. Therefore stay awake—for you do not know when the master of the house will come, in the evening, or at midnight, or when the rooster crows, or in the morning—lest he come suddenly and find you asleep. And what I say to you I say to all: Stay awake."

Reflect:

In Mark 13, time was short for Jesus's earthly ministry. This passage on the end of things was Jesus's last teaching before the Lord's Supper and Passion. We do not know when the Lord will come to make all things new. In the words of Saint Paul, now we see through a glass darkly, but then we shall see face-to-face. Jesus said, "But concerning that day or that hour, no one knows, not even the angels in heaven, nor the Son, but only the Father. Be on guard, keep awake. For you do not know when the time will come" (vv. 32–33).

Spending our energy on trying to predict the future isn't productive or helpful. Jesus encouraged us instead to "stay awake"—making ourselves, our families, and our communities ready for the kingdom of God.

What does it mean to "stay awake"?

It means faithfully living according to the faithfulness of God in Jesus Christ. It does not mean hoarding food in our basements; on the contrary, it means sharing it with the food bank or neighbors in need.

It means allowing the hope of the gospel to completely transform one's imagination, longings, and vocation. It means letting the love of God illumine one's heart and animate one's life, even when the earth quakes and the seas roar.

One day all things will become clear, and we will stand in the fullness of God's kingdom. Until that day, three things remain—faith, hope, and love.

As you pray, ask the Lord for steadfast love, for trust in his providence, and for the ability to keep awake until his return.

Pray:

O gladsome light,
pure brightness of the everliving Father in heaven,
O Jesus Christ, holy and blessed!
Now as we come to the setting of the sun,
and our eyes behold the vesper light,
we sing your praises, O God: Father, Son, and Holy Spirit.
You are worthy at all times to be praised by happy voices,
O Son of God, O Giver of Life,
and to be glorified through all the worlds.
Amen.

(Anglican Church in North America Book of Common Prayer)

Introduction to Holy Week
STEVEN E. BREEDLOVE

*H*OLY WEEK OFFERS US THE CHANCE to enter into the life of Christ. We wave palm branches; we celebrate the Last Supper and wash each other's feet; we place crosses in our churches, sometimes kneeling before them; we fast on Saturday, perhaps waiting in vigil that evening; and then we break forth in joy and celebration on Easter morning. Over the course of this week, the life of Christ—the specific things he did and said, and the things done to him dominates our devotions and worship.

This is as it should be, for our hope is grounded in the life, death, and resurrection of Christ. Our growth in the faith must also revolve around this. We need an annual tradition to rehearse and reenter the foundation of our faith. During this week, we are given the chance to center our life on Christ in an explicit way and let our prayers respond to what he did that week.

On Palm Sunday, as we cheer with the throngs, our prayers should be, "Hosanna! Save us, Son of David!" From Monday to Wednesday, as we read the final words Jesus spoke in the temple, our prayers should be, "Lord, examine me. May I be built on you, my cornerstone!" On Thursday, we should meditate on the washing of feet, marvel at the Last Supper, and pray that we too would love one another and be preserved when our faith is tested. We should grieve in prayer with the Lord as we ponder Gethsemane, asking that we might stay awake in prayer during temptation. And on Friday, a day that can only be called "good" because on it our redemption was purchased, the cost of our life should drive us to prayers of both sorrow and joy.

Yet when Sunday comes, our prayers should become victory songs—not merely joyous, but fully triumphant—as we remember the resurrection of the Lord. Come, Lord Jesus!

Palm Sunday

SALLY BREEDLOVE

Read: *Matthew 21:1–5*

Now when they drew near to Jerusalem and came to Bethphage, to
the Mount of Olives, then Jesus sent two disciples, saying to them,
"Go into the village in front of you, and immediately you will find a
donkey tied, and a colt with her. Untie them and bring them to me.
If anyone says anything to you, you shall say, 'The Lord needs them,'
and he will send them at once." This took place to fulfill what was
spoken by the prophet, saying,

"Say to the daughter of Zion,
'Behold, your king is coming to you,
humble, and mounted on a donkey,
on a colt, the foal of a beast of burden.'"

Reflect:

On Palm Sunday we celebrate Christ's triumphal entry into Jerusalem. Today
is only a pause on the road to the cross, but it resounds with meaning. Jesus
is the humble King. As John 12:15 tells us, we no longer have to be afraid. As
Mark 11:10 reminds us, the coming kingdom of our father David is blessed.

But pause with Jesus one more time on that high place of the Mount of
Olives, look down into the Kidron Valley, and then lift your eyes to see the
city of Jerusalem. Jesus had to descend and then climb before he entered the
Holy City. Is this panorama a vision of the real descent he would make, the
walk through the valley of death that led to the cross?

On that morning, how did he endure the thought of all that lay ahead?
Hebrews 12:2 declares that the joy set before him strengthened him. That
passage concludes with this encouragement to us: Our ultimate destination
is the city of joy, which cannot be shaken, the city where all who belong to
God are gathered together.

Listen: You've come to Mount Zion, the city where the living God
resides. The invisible Jerusalem is populated by throngs of festive angels and

Christian citizens. It is the city where God is Judge, with judgments that make us just. You've come to Jesus, who presented us with a new covenant, a fresh charter from God. He is the Mediator of this covenant. The murder of Jesus, unlike Abel's—a homicide that cried out for vengeance—became a proclamation of grace:

> "So don't turn a deaf ear to these gracious words.... Do you see what we've got? An unshakable kingdom! And do you see how thankful we must be? Not only thankful, but brimming with worship, deeply reverent before God." (Hebrews 12:25, 28 MSG)

What lies ahead of us? Perhaps a deeper descent into the valley of suffering—but even if this is so, we are never abandoned there. As Psalm 23:4 reminds us, in the darkest valley, the truth is still the truth. Christ is Immanuel, God with us, no matter where the road leads.

He is indeed leading us to the city that endures forever, the New Jerusalem, which will come down from heaven. His alone is the unshakable kingdom, the dwelling place of joy, where God wipes away every tear, heals every disease, dispels every fear, and makes all things new. We can endure.

Pray:

Almighty and everlasting God, in your tender love you sent your Son, our Savior Jesus Christ, to take on our flesh and to suffer death upon the cross for our sins. Mercifully grant us to join in his resurrection from the dead by the power of the Holy Spirit and to follow him all our days. Give patience and strength to those who are serving others during these days of hardship. Bring comfort to those who are suffering and let all turn unto you for everlasting life. Amen.

(Adapted from Anglican Church in North America Book of Common Prayer)

Monday of Holy Week
SALLY BREEDLOVE

Read: *John 12:20–28*

> Now among those who went up to worship at the feast were some Greeks. So these came to Philip, who was from Bethsaida in Galilee, and asked him, "Sir, we wish to see Jesus." Philip went and told Andrew; Andrew and Philip went and told Jesus. And Jesus answered them, "The hour has come for the Son of Man to be glorified. Truly, truly, I say to you, unless a grain of wheat falls into the earth and dies, it remains alone; but if it dies, it bears much fruit. Whoever loves his life loses it, and whoever hates his life in this world will keep it for eternal life. If anyone serves me, he must follow me; and where I am, there will my servant be also. If anyone serves me, the Father will honor him.
>
> "Now is my soul troubled. And what shall I say? 'Father, save me from this hour'? But for this purpose I have come to this hour. Father, glorify your name." Then a voice came from heaven: "I have glorified it, and I will glorify it again."

Reflect:

Jesus had entered Jerusalem in triumph, but the acclamation he received just days prior was deteriorating. The Jewish leaders who served as enforcers for Roman rule had decided that Jesus must die. In that context, the story of Greeks wanting to meet Jesus seems like a sidebar event, not one to make the front page. But in truth, it is the real story. Jesus's mission is so large, and God's compassion for all the world is so great, that the Jewish nation could not contain it any longer. It spilled over to the Gentiles.

This is good and sobering news. Christ knew this outpouring of God's mercy required his own death. He said, "Now is my soul troubled. And what shall I say? 'Father, save me from this hour'? But for this purpose I have come to this hour" (v. 27).

Rather than explaining his coming crucifixion in this passage, Christ illustrated it. A seed has to be put in the ground and die, or else it will never be more than a seed. But if it dies, it reproduces itself. In the world of farming, one wheat kernel planted in the ground gives birth to between three and five hundred new seeds. Jesus knew his death would open the door to life for countless others.

As Christ continued in John 12, he turned the focus to us: "In the same way, anyone who holds on to life just as it is destroys that life. But if you let it go, reckless in your love, you'll have it forever, real and eternal. If any of you wants to serve me, then follow me" (John 12:25–26 MSG).

Do we insist on holding our life as it has been? None of us has the power to keep our lives from changing. What would it be like to live a life of reckless love, following Jesus wherever he leads us?

Will you pray for your own willingness to follow Jesus into this chaotic and deteriorating world? Will you let die what he asks you to let die? Will you ask him to help you love like he loves? Will you give your fears and sadness to him?

Pray. We are up against more than we can solve on our own, but the mighty, eternal God is with us.

Pray:

Lord Jesus Christ, thank you for this time to praise your name and call upon you for help. There are many hurting right now, not only where we live but also around the world. Please bring your swift rescue to the sick, the sorrowful, and the wounded. We know that there are places you want to reign in our lives, but we are reluctant to let you step in. We look to you for help and salvation. Deliver us from our desire to control our world. We look to you for rescue, and we declare you to be Lord of our lives. Please save us. Amen.

Tuesday of Holy Week
BRANDON WALSH

Read: *Mark 14:17–25*

And when it was evening, he came with the twelve. And as they were reclining at table and eating, Jesus said, "Truly, I say to you, one of you will betray me, one who is eating with me." They began to be sorrowful and to say to him one after another, "Is it I?" He said to them, "It is one of the twelve, one who is dipping bread into the dish with me. For the Son of Man goes as it is written of him, but woe to that man by whom the Son of Man is betrayed! It would have been better for that man if he had not been born."

And as they were eating, he took bread, and after blessing it broke it and gave it to them, and said, "Take; this is my body." And he took a cup, and when he had given thanks he gave it to them, and they all drank of it. And he said to them, "This is my blood of the covenant, which is poured out for many. Truly, I say to you, I will not drink again of the fruit of the vine until that day when I drink it new in the kingdom of God."

Reflect:

The word *companion* comes from two Latin words and literally means "with bread." A companion is one with whom you share bread. When Jesus and his disciples celebrated this final meal, this Last Supper, they had been through so much. Jesus, the miracle worker, had calmed the sea, raised the dead, humbled the proud, and exalted the humble. Hopes and ambitions alike kindled in the disciples' hearts. A Messiah, a King, a Lord: All the lights of prophetic hope were focused on Jesus as if through a magnifying glass.

Jesus took bread, blessed it, and broke it. He lifted a cup, gave thanks, and offered it. He would be broken like the bread. He would be poured out like the wine.

Jesus took twelve men and made them companions, but more than that, he broke his body to make all of us companions with God. We who walked in darkness have seen a great light—not primarily in heavenly splendor but in ordinary bread and wine. God has come near to us and continues to invite us to his table to be his companions. Remember Christ as you break bread at your dinner table. Give thanks for his goodness when you drink from your cup. Call to mind his sacrifice when you next take communion.

As you pray, rejoice that Jesus is our companion now and always.

Pray:

Dear Jesus, I believe that you are truly present in the Holy Sacrament. I love you above all things, and I desire to possess you within my soul. And since I cannot now receive you sacramentally, I beseech you to come spiritually into my heart. I unite myself to you, together with all your faithful people gathered around every altar of your Church, and I embrace you with all the affections of my soul. Never permit me to be separated from you. Amen.

(Anglican Church in North America Book of Common Prayer)

Wednesday of Holy Week
PHIL ASHEY

Read: *Luke 22:39–53*

And he came out and went, as was his custom, to the Mount of Olives, and the disciples followed him. And when he came to the place, he said to them, "Pray that you may not enter into temptation." And he withdrew from them about a stone's throw, and knelt down and prayed, saying, "Father, if you are willing, remove this cup from me. Nevertheless, not my will, but yours, be done." And there appeared to him an angel from heaven, strengthening him. And being in agony he prayed more earnestly; and his sweat became like great drops of blood falling down to the ground. And when he rose from prayer, he came to the disciples and found them sleeping for sorrow, and he said to them, "Why are you sleeping? Rise and pray that you may not enter into temptation."

While he was still speaking, there came a crowd, and the man called Judas, one of the twelve, was leading them. He drew near to Jesus to kiss him, but Jesus said to him, "Judas, would you betray the Son of Man with a kiss?" And when those who were around him saw what would follow, they said, "Lord, shall we strike with the sword?" And one of them struck the servant of the high priest and cut off his right ear. But Jesus said, "No more of this!" And he touched his ear and healed him. Then Jesus said to the chief priests and officers of the temple and elders, who had come out against him, "Have you come out as against a robber, with swords and clubs? When I was with you day after day in the temple, you did not lay hands on me. But this is your hour, and the power of darkness."

Reflect:

Jesus faced a dark hour in a dark night in the garden of Gethsemane. He faced it as he so often did, in prayer; only this time he labored until he sweated drops of blood. This detail alone speaks volumes about the spiritual, physical, and emotional burden that Jesus carried as he faced crucifixion. It is a vivid picture of the humanity of Jesus in the midst of his divine obedience. Here, darkness fell. Jesus faced anxiety and fear, dread of his impending crucifixion, grief, weariness, friends letting him down in his hour of need, betrayal, and the temptation to take a swing and fight back.

How do we pray when the darkness descends and we cannot see light or life on the other side? Gethsemane may come to us as an unwelcome diagnosis of a life-threatening disease, the loss of a job, betrayal by a friend, or some other grievous loss. What can we learn from Jesus about how to face such deep difficulty?

Jesus entered this hour of utter darkness in a posture that was familiar to him—a posture of prayer. When the darkness falls for us, we pray as Jesus did, not allowing the crisis to consume us, as the disciples did, but rather allowing it to drive us to our knees. Like Jesus, we face both the facts before us and our feelings. They may be desperate, but we give voice to both in prayer just as Jesus did.

Only God could show Jesus the way forward through the onslaught of hell itself. Jesus did not surrender or submit to the reign of darkness. Rather, he surrendered and submitted to his Father: "Nevertheless, not my will, but yours, be done" (v. 42).

Are you ready to pray as simply and as intimately as Jesus prayed: "Father, what do you want?" Are you ready and willing to surrender yourself to the path the Father has set down before you? Are you ready to entrust yourself to the Father just as Jesus did and to receive the same strength he received from heaven?

Pray:

Dear Lord and Savior Jesus Christ: I hold up all my weakness to your strength, my failure to your faithfulness, my sinfulness to your perfection, my loneliness to your compassion, my little pains to your great agony on the Cross. I pray that you will cleanse me, strengthen me, guide me so that in all ways my life may be lived as you would have it lived, without cowardice and for you alone. Show me how to live in true humility, true contrition, and true love. Amen.

(Anglican Church in North America Book of Common Prayer)

Maundy Thursday

PHIL ASHEY

Read: *Luke 22:54–62*

> Then they seized him and led him away, bringing him into the high priest's house, and Peter was following at a distance. And when they had kindled a fire in the middle of the courtyard and sat down together, Peter sat down among them. Then a servant girl, seeing him as he sat in the light and looking closely at him, said, "This man also was with him." But he denied it, saying, "Woman, I do not know him." And a little later someone else saw him and said, "You also are one of them." But Peter said, "Man, I am not." And after an interval of about an hour still another insisted, saying, "Certainly this man also was with him, for he too is a Galilean." But Peter said, "Man, I do not know what you are talking about." And immediately, while he was still speaking, the rooster crowed. And the Lord turned and looked at Peter. And Peter remembered the saying of the Lord, how he had said to him, "Before the rooster crows today, you will deny me three times." And he went out and wept bitterly.

Reflect:

Peter failed. After following Jesus closely for three years, he followed Jesus at a distance. Under peer pressure, physical distance gave way to emotional distance, emotional distance gave way to emphatic denial, and that denial finally gave way to cursing and swearing (Matthew 26:74). When Jesus turned at that final denial and looked straight at Peter, all Peter could remember were Jesus's words, "You will deny me" (Matthew 26:34). In that moment, Peter realized he was a complete disappointment.

How do we pray in the face of our failures, our following Jesus at a distance, and the conviction that we, too, have denied him in word and deed?

There is another side to failure: There we find grace and forgiveness, redemption and restoration, hope and a future in Christ alone. We remember that "weeping may tarry for the night, but joy comes with the morning" (Psalm 30:5).

We remember that Jesus had more words for Peter than "You will deny me." Jesus prepared Peter for the sifting he would experience by Satan, the loss of his faith, and the restoration of his leadership (Luke 22:31–32). Knowing Peter's heart, Jesus did restore him (John 21:15–19) in a threefold consecration, redeeming each one of Peter's denials. In Acts 2, Peter was not only restored and redeemed but was also filled with the Holy Spirit in order to faithfully proclaim Christ to all the nations.

The resurrection of Jesus Christ vindicated every promise Jesus ever made to Peter and every promise he makes to you and me. We too can live with hope on the other side of our failures. Let the story of Peter's denial and restoration open your eyes to the redemption and restoration Christ has for all of us through his resurrection power. Let us pray with thanksgiving as Peter did.

Pray:

Almighty God and Father, we praise you for sending your Son Jesus Christ to die on the cross for all our sins. By your great mercy, we have been born anew to a living hope through the resurrection of Jesus Christ from the dead. By your Holy Spirit, strengthen our faith so that in this life we may possess the fullness of that living hope and that in the life to come we may possess our imperishable, undefiled, and unfading inheritance in Christ. Through him who reigns with you and the Holy Spirit, one God, now and forever! Amen.

(Adapted from 1 Peter 1:3–5)

Good Friday

PHIL ASHEY

Read: *Luke 23:1–5, 13–25*

Then the whole company of them arose and brought him before Pilate. And they began to accuse him, saying, "We found this man misleading our nation and forbidding us to give tribute to Caesar, and saying that he himself is Christ, a king." And Pilate asked him, "Are you the King of the Jews?" And he answered him, "You have said so." Then Pilate said to the chief priests and the crowds, "I find no guilt in this man." But they were urgent, saying, "He stirs up the people, teaching throughout all Judea, from Galilee even to this place."…

Pilate then called together the chief priests and the rulers and the people, and said to them, "You brought me this man as one who was misleading the people. And after examining him before you, behold, I did not find this man guilty of any of your charges against him. Neither did Herod, for he sent him back to us. Look, nothing deserving death has been done by him. I will therefore punish and release him."

But they all cried out together, "Away with this man, and release to us Barabbas"—a man who had been thrown into prison for an insurrection started in the city and for murder. Pilate addressed them once more, desiring to release Jesus, but they kept shouting, "Crucify, crucify him!" A third time he said to them, "Why? What evil has he done? I have found in him no guilt deserving death. I will therefore punish and release him." But they were urgent, demanding with loud cries that he should be crucified. And their voices prevailed. So Pilate decided that their demand should be granted. He released the man who had been thrown into prison for insurrection and murder, for whom they asked, but he delivered Jesus over to their will.

Reflect:

We possess a natural human need to have the last word. Have you noticed how often online comments degenerate into arguments that are never-ending because every person feels the need to get in the last word on the matter at hand?

In this passage, Jesus surrendered his right to have the last word. Politics, personalities, and unjust legal proceedings swirled about him. Herod plied him with many questions, but Jesus "made no answer" (v. 9). Pilate questioned him again and again, and when asked, "Are you the King of the Jews?" Jesus barely replied, "You have said so" (v. 3). Jesus was assaulted by false and vehement accusations, personal ridicule, mocking, and eventually, shouts of "Crucify, crucify him!" (v. 21) that overpowered the evidence of his innocence. Jesus did not defend himself. "When they hurled their insults at him, he did not retaliate; when he suffered, he made no threats. Instead, he entrusted himself to him who judges justly" (1 Peter 2:23 NIV).

Through Christ, God's supreme act of love for you and me was to suffer a gross miscarriage of justice silently, surrendering his right to have the last word. We know the end of the story—that in Christ and his resurrection, God still has the last word. But in this moment Jesus manifested God's love for the world in silence, surrendering his right to have the last word this side of the cross and suffering the greatest injustice of all.

Following Jesus means that we will also "share his sufferings" (Philippians 3:10). Is God calling you in Christ to exercise that discipline of silence, just as Jesus did, in the face of criticism, a false accusation, or even gross injustice? How will you pray as you share in the fellowship of Jesus's silence?

Pray:

Almighty God, whose most dear Son went not up to joy but first he suffered pain, and entered not into glory before he was crucified: Mercifully grant that we, walking in the way of the Cross, may find it none other than the way of life and peace; through Jesus Christ your Son our Lord. Amen.

(Anglican Church in North America Book of Common Prayer)

Holy Saturday
PHIL ASHEY

Read: *Luke 23:32–35, 44–46*

Two others, who were criminals, were led away to be put to death with him. And when they came to the place that is called The Skull, there they crucified him, and the criminals, one on his right and one on his left. And Jesus said, "Father, forgive them, for they know not what they do." And they cast lots to divide his garments. And the people stood by, watching, but the rulers scoffed at him, saying, "He saved others; let him save himself, if he is the Christ of God, his Chosen One!"...

It was now about the sixth hour, and there was darkness over the whole land until the ninth hour, while the sun's light failed. And the curtain of the temple was torn in two. Then Jesus, calling out with a loud voice, said, "Father, into your hands I commit my spirit!" And having said this he breathed his last.

Reflect:

Imagine your dying declaration. What would you choose to say? A goodbye to loved ones? A blessing on them? An expression of awe at the prospect of heaven that you are now approaching?

Jesus's final words from the cross were simply the summation of the way he lived his life. The breakers of death were about to roll over him. He was so near death that he was no longer attentive to anything but his own Spirit. He was not preaching. He was not trying to convince anyone. These words expressed his heart; they were between Jesus and the Father alone.

These words are a prayer from Psalm 31:5, which every Jewish mother taught her little children to pray before drifting off to sleep. But Jesus added to it one little word: *Abba*, meaning "father." "Father, into your hands I commit my spirit!" (v. 46). In the midst of his abandonment, Jesus spoke this personal, intimate prayer from his heart to the Father. Hell itself could not invade that place!

Jesus was convinced that Father God was waiting for him with open arms. He trusted in the Father's goodness, plans, and wisdom, which dwarfed all fears of the unknown. He calmly, voluntarily, and intentionally released his life into the Father's hands. Finally, he cried out with a loud voice—not a feeble, whimpering surrender, but a great and victorious embrace: "Father, into your hands I commit my spirit!"

In his dying prayer, Jesus gave us a model for hope. We believe in a God who overcomes death, who provides hope to the hopeless and heals the brokenhearted. In reality, we cannot fix, cure, or heal anyone or anything. Only God can do that.

Is there someone in your life, perhaps even you yourself, who needs healing? Is there something in your life that needs to be restored? Can you pray as Jesus did with a passionate trust in and abandonment to God for that restoration? Will you entrust yourself and your loved ones to your heavenly Father?

Pray:

O God of the living, on this day your Son our Savior descended to the place of the dead: Look with kindness on all of us who wait in hope for liberation from the corruption of sin and death, and give us a share in the glory of the children of God; through Jesus Christ your Son our Lord. Amen.

(Anglican Church in North America Book of Common Prayer)

Introduction to Eastertide
STEVEN E. BREEDLOVE

OR THE DISCIPLES who encountered Jesus between his resurrection and ascension, forty days likely felt far too short. After his crucifixion and resurrection, there were so many questions to ask, and every moment with the risen Lord was precious. Yet today the Easter season may seem incredibly long. How can we sustain resurrection joy for the seven weeks between Resurrection Sunday and Pentecost? If it's difficult to celebrate for twelve days at Christmas, how much more difficult is it to celebrate through the whole Easter season? Perhaps this difficulty is partially connected to our inability to prepare.

In order for celebration to fit into our souls, we need preparation. Celebration will always be in proportion to the depth of the preparation. Perhaps this is why those Christian traditions that practice Lent most deeply also seem to celebrate Easter most richly.

But there is more going on here. Fixing our eyes on the resurrection—the firstfruits of all things being made new, the testimony of our own future in Christ, the shattering of all that is evil and grievous in the world—is hard to do. We run out of steam because what we are celebrating is at odds with what we experience in the world. Celebration will come easy in the new heavens and earth because our experience will finally be in accord with reality.

Yet we can still learn to pray in accord with Easter, and the resurrection can still undergird our prayers. We can devote ourselves to prayers that assume that the corruptible will be made incorruptible, and the perishable made imperishable, even if in our doubt we struggle to comprehend what this will ultimately mean. This is as straightforward as acknowledging the brokenness and death in the world, and stating to the Lord, "Yet this, too, is not your final word, for the resurrection is coming!" It is as simple as asking our risen King, "Would you raise me up in this struggle even as I wait for the day when death is swallowed up in victory?"

Resurrection Sunday

PHIL ASHEY

Read: *Luke 24:1–12*

> But on the first day of the week, at early dawn, they went to the tomb, taking the spices they had prepared. And they found the stone rolled away from the tomb, but when they went in they did not find the body of the Lord Jesus. While they were perplexed about this, behold, two men stood by them in dazzling apparel. And as they were frightened and bowed their faces to the ground, the men said to them, "Why do you seek the living among the dead? He is not here, but has risen. Remember how he told you, while he was still in Galilee, that the Son of Man must be delivered into the hands of sinful men and be crucified and on the third day rise." And they remembered his words, and returning from the tomb they told all these things to the eleven and to all the rest. Now it was Mary Magdalene and Joanna and Mary the mother of James and the other women with them who told these things to the apostles, but these words seemed to them an idle tale, and they did not believe them. But Peter rose and ran to the tomb; stooping and looking in, he saw the linen cloths by themselves; and he went home marveling at what had happened.

Reflect:

The last thing the women expected to find that morning was the stone rolled away from the tomb. They had seen Jesus's body laid in the tomb; they had come to anoint his body with the spices they had prepared. Their faith's entire frame of reference had been collapsed by the stark and brutal reality of Jesus's death. The huge, heavy stone rolled across the tomb was a physical sign of the impossible situation they faced. Jesus was dead and decaying in that stone-cold tomb, and with him their hopes and dreams had also perished.

What impossible and uncontrollable reality are you facing in your life today? What burden too heavy to bear, what situation too impossible to move, what mistake or hurt so costly that it has entombed your hopes? What is out of control in your life—with your children, your health, your job, your finances? What habits are you trying to break but failing to do so, no matter how hard you try? What is it in your life that you'd like to change but you find yourself unable to alter?

Listen to the good news Luke proclaimed from that resurrection morning. When everything seemed out of control, when a hope and a future seemed impossible, after hours and hours of living with powerlessness, these women were jolted out of the impossible by the rolled-away stone and the words of the angels: "Why do you seek the living among the dead? He is not here, but has risen" (v. 5).

The resurrection of Jesus means that God has the power to roll away the impossibilities in our lives. As you pray, remember that the same resurrection power that raised Jesus from the dead is the power God offers us in Christ. It is the power Jesus promised his followers long before he died, when he said to them, "With man it is impossible, but not with God. For all things are possible with God" (Mark 10:27).

Pray:

Almighty God, I ask you to give me the spirit of wisdom and revelation so that I might know you better. Enlighten the eyes of my heart in order that I may know your hope, the riches of your glorious inheritance, and your incomparably great power for believers. May the same power that you exerted in raising Jesus from the dead be at work in my life, my family, my workplace, and my community, to roll away the impossibles, so that Christ himself will be exalted; through Jesus Christ our Lord. Amen.

(Adapted from Ephesians 1:15–22)

Monday of Easter Week

SALLY BREEDLOVE

Read: *Revelation 21:1–8*

Then I saw a new heaven and a new earth, for the first heaven and the first earth had passed away, and the sea was no more. And I saw the holy city, new Jerusalem, coming down out of heaven from God, prepared as a bride adorned for her husband. And I heard a loud voice from the throne saying, "Behold, the dwelling place of God is with man. He will dwell with them, and they will be his people, and God himself will be with them as their God. He will wipe away every tear from their eyes, and death shall be no more, neither shall there be mourning, nor crying, nor pain anymore, for the former things have passed away."

And he who was seated on the throne said, "Behold, I am making all things new." Also he said, "Write this down, for these words are trustworthy and true." And he said to me, "It is done! I am the Alpha and the Omega, the beginning and the end. To the thirsty I will give from the spring of the water of life without payment. The one who conquers will have this heritage, and I will be his God and he will be my son. But as for the cowardly, the faithless, the detestable, as for murderers, the sexually immoral, sorcerers, idolaters, and all liars, their portion will be in the lake that burns with fire and sulfur, which is the second death."

Reflect:

The resurrection of Jesus broke apart the old, inevitable cycle of death. That very first Easter evening, the resurrected Christ made himself visible and recognizable to Mary, to his friends walking the Emmaus road, and to his locked-in-a-room-in-fear disciples.

And now it is Easter Monday, a day to breathe a sigh of relief. Christians sometimes call Easter Sunday "the eighth day." That eighth day is not just one day, however—it is the name for all time after the resurrection of Jesus.

We no longer live in the old creation with its seven days repeating themselves over and over again. We live instead in the new order.

In times like ours, this new order of reality may often seem dim. The world is still broken by sin. We still suffer. Life is not as it should be. But while these things are true, they are not all that is or all that will be.

The real and ultimate truth is the future that Revelation 21 paints. The earth will be remade and restored, and the barrier between heaven and earth will be removed.

Will you choose to live as an eighth-day person in a world staggering with troubles? The promises God has given us are real. Will you learn them by heart and not just with your head?

No matter how deeply death and grief have touched you, the eighth day has arrived. Will you accept both—the reality of the world you live in and the goodness of Christ's coming reign on earth?

As you pray, take time to speak aloud what you most look forward to in that eighth-day world. Pray in thanksgiving for what is already true and what will one day arrive in fullness.

Pray for those who grieve. Pray that alongside their grief, they may experience a sure sense of the hope that lies ahead. Pray they are comforted and strengthened by the risen Christ.

Pray:

This is the day that the Lord has made. We will rejoice and be glad in it! O Lord, we thank you that we are alive now in a new world. We see the passing of sin and death, and we taste the fruit of Christ's resurrection. We are hurting and we lament as we behold the toll of this world's falling away from you. Yet we rejoice as we rest, seeing how you have pursued us and will never let us go. Please comfort the afflicted. Give them tender relief and hope in your salvation. Preserve us and help us never to forget what you have already done. Amen.

Tuesday of Easter Week
SALLY BREEDLOVE

Read: *Luke 24:15–27, 31–32*

While they were talking and discussing together, Jesus himself drew near and went with them. But their eyes were kept from recognizing him. And he said to them, "What is this conversation that you are holding with each other as you walk?" And they stood still, looking sad. Then one of them, named Cleopas, answered him, "Are you the only visitor to Jerusalem who does not know the things that have happened there in these days?" And he said to them, "What things?" And they said to him, "Concerning Jesus of Nazareth, a man who was a prophet mighty in deed and word before God and all the people, and how our chief priests and rulers delivered him up to be condemned to death, and crucified him. But we had hoped that he was the one to redeem Israel. Yes, and besides all this, it is now the third day since these things happened. Moreover, some women of our company amazed us. They were at the tomb early in the morning, and when they did not find his body, they came back saying that they had even seen a vision of angels, who said that he was alive. Some of those who were with us went to the tomb and found it just as the women had said, but him they did not see." And he said to them, "O foolish ones, and slow of heart to believe all that the prophets have spoken! Was it not necessary that the Christ should suffer these things and enter into his glory?" And beginning with Moses and all the Prophets, he interpreted to them in all the Scriptures the things concerning himself....

And their eyes were opened, and they recognized him. And he vanished from their sight. They said to each other, "Did not our hearts burn within us while he talked to us on the road, while he opened to us the Scriptures?"

Reflect:

What can we learn from those followers of Jesus who walked the road to Emmaus? What habits of the heart and what choices shaped their ability to recognize him?

The two on that road were honest. They let their confusion and grief speak. They wondered about the things Jesus had said and what the women who went to the tomb witnessed. They didn't run from what they were experiencing.

Are you willing to tell the truth about your own confusion, frustration, and fears? Will you turn away from the temptation to fill hard times with endless distractions? A plasticized Christianity of perfect belief will not stand the test of trial. A distracted life will reap no harvest from the hard things you endure.

Second, these two listened to the Scriptures and to the stranger with curiosity. They didn't assume they already knew the answers. God wants us to turn to him and turn to his Word. He wants our humility and our willingness to be taught. Will you admit you don't know everything? Will you ponder? Are you willing to listen and obey?

Finally, these two welcomed the stranger. Like Mary, who was willing to ask the gardener for help, the Emmaus pair turned toward the stranger on the road with them. Are you willing to be open to those around you and to see the presence of Christ in unexpected people?

It's Eastertide, seven weeks of joy spilling out until Pentecost. Good news has come, Christ died to atone for all sin, and God has raised him from the dead. Life has the final word. We can rejoice that we are not alone.

Pray for yourself. Pray you will let go of your presumptions. Pray for the humility to be honest, to listen to the Word with new ears, and to receive the stranger. Pray you have eyes to see Christ. He is here.

Pray:

O Lord, soften our hearts and open our ears to hear afresh the good news that you have conquered the grave. May your name be glorified above all names as you are our worthy God and King. Please be at work in us. Show us how to love our neighbors in acts of service and steady prayer. Amen.

Wednesday of Easter Week

MADISON PERRY

Read: *Luke 24:36–43, 50–53*

> As they were talking about these things, Jesus himself stood among
> them, and said to them, "Peace to you!" But they were startled
> and frightened and thought they saw a spirit. And he said to them,
> "Why are you troubled, and why do doubts arise in your hearts? See
> my hands and my feet, that it is I myself. Touch me, and see. For
> a spirit does not have flesh and bones as you see that I have." And
> when he had said this, he showed them his hands and his feet. And
> while they still disbelieved for joy and were marveling, he said to
> them, "Have you anything here to eat?" They gave him a piece of
> broiled fish, and he took it and ate before them....
>
> And he led them out as far as Bethany, and lifting up his hands
> he blessed them. While he blessed them, he parted from them and
> was carried up into heaven. And they worshiped him and returned
> to Jerusalem with great joy, and were continually in the temple
> blessing God.

Reflect:

This is the end of Luke's Gospel. The most important event in history has
occurred: Jesus has been resurrected from the dead.

If this were a story written by humans, Jesus would immediately assume
power. Justice would roll down. History would accelerate to its end. Peace
and prosperity would ensue.

Yet the revolution we would expect didn't explode into motion. After
conquering the grave, Jesus encountered his disciples in gentle ways. He
didn't demand apologies or cow them by revelations of his glory and splendor.
He approached them and waited for them to understand. When they were
troubled, he showed them his scars. He noted that he was hungry and asked
for food. Then without warning, Jesus "parted from them and was carried up
into heaven. And they worshiped him and returned to Jerusalem with great
joy, and were continually in the temple blessing God" (vv. 51–52).

Instead of full resolution, we are given relational reconciliation, the sharing of food, and the worship of God. These are the crucial things we still need to prioritize.

God does not need us for his revolution—and his revolution has not paused. Jesus reigns and will reign forever, even in the midst of our unresolved pain and our lingering questions. What a privilege that we can be drawn into heavenly worship by the Holy Spirit.

So now, wherever you are, turn to God in praise: "*Holy, holy, holy is the* LORD *of hosts; the whole earth is full of his glory!*" (Isaiah 6:3). Proclaim this to God several times. As you do so, you edge into eternity. Ask him that his kingdom would come, that his will would be done on earth as it is in heaven. Trust that there will be earthly resolution. We have known Christ's resurrection life, and one day it will also fill our bodies and brokenness. If you do not feel joy, consider praising God until you sense a measure of peace.

Pray:

Praise the LORD, my soul.
LORD my God, you are very great;
  you are clothed with splendor and majesty.
The LORD wraps himself in light as with a garment;
  he stretches out the heavens like a tent
  and lays the beams of his upper chambers on their waters.
He makes the clouds his chariot
  and rides on the wings of the wind.
He makes winds his messengers,
  flames of fire his servants....
May the glory of the LORD endure forever;
  may the LORD rejoice in his works—
Amen.

(Psalm 104:1–4, 31 NIV*)*

Thursday of Easter Week
SALLY BREEDLOVE

Read: *Revelation 1:12–18*

Then I turned to see the voice that was speaking to me, and on turning I saw seven golden lampstands, and in the midst of the lampstands one like a son of man, clothed with a long robe and with a golden sash around his chest. The hairs of his head were white, like white wool, like snow. His eyes were like a flame of fire, his feet were like burnished bronze, refined in a furnace, and his voice was like the roar of many waters. In his right hand he held seven stars, from his mouth came a sharp two-edged sword, and his face was like the sun shining in full strength.

When I saw him, I fell at his feet as though dead. But he laid his right hand on me, saying, "Fear not, I am the first and the last, and the living one. I died, and behold I am alive forevermore, and I have the keys of Death and Hades."

Reflect:

Does it seem to you as if good news hasn't made the headlines in a very long time? Perhaps on a personal level you've experienced blessings—but corporate good news? It can feel as though it doesn't exist.

But at the birth of Christ, we discover extravagant promise after extravagant promise declared by people and angels: A brilliant future was in store where longings would be met, mercy poured out, the strong shamed, the downtrodden exalted, and those sitting in fear and the shadow of death visited by the sunrise from on high. Those promises were so plentiful they jumbled together. Perhaps they are best summed up in the words the angels declared to the shepherds the night Christ was born: "Good news of great joy for all people."

And yet for the thirty-something years of Jesus's life, corporate good news was still scarce. Yes, Jesus healed, raised some from the dead, released others from demonic bondage, extended forgiveness, calmed storms, and fed thousands. But none of that touched everyone, and none of it lasted. And then he was crucified. It was over.

Except it wasn't. The promises had taken root. We are in Eastertide, celebrating Jesus's resurrection. The good news of great joy for all people has been accomplished. Death no longer rules; the indestructible life of Jesus saves us to the uttermost.

The Lamb who was slain and who now lives forever as the eternal Son at the Father's right hand has met our deepest longing with extravagant abundance. He is the First and the Last. He is the Living One; he was dead, and now look—he is alive forever and ever!

He invites you to trust him. Will you do that? Let your prayers today be of praise, adoration, and thanksgiving.

Pray:

Our heavenly Father, we praise your name! You have caused us to be born again to a living hope by the resurrection of Jesus Christ from the dead. For surely we were once dead—our hearts were barren, our sin was great, our betrayal of you was undeniable. Yet you took on yourself our weakness and treason, and in your tender mercy from on high you gave us your only begotten Son. And so now we pray as did your servant Simeon: Sovereign Lord, you may now dismiss your servant in peace. For my eyes have seen your salvation, which you have prepared in the sight of all nations: a light for revelation to the Gentiles and the glory of your people Israel. Hallelujah. Amen.

Friday of Easter Week
ELIZABETH GATEWOOD

Read: *Hosea 2:16–20*

"And in that day, declares the LORD, you will call me 'My Husband,' and no longer will you call me 'My Baal.' For I will remove the names of the Baals from her mouth, and they shall be remembered by name no more. And I will make for them a covenant on that day with the beasts of the field, the birds of the heavens, and the creeping things of the ground. And I will abolish the bow, the sword, and war from the land, and I will make you lie down in safety. And I will betroth you to me forever. I will betroth you to me in righteousness and in justice, in steadfast love and in mercy. I will betroth you to me in faithfulness. And you shall know the LORD."

Reflect:

God is a relentless lover. In the book of Hosea, God commanded Hosea to bind himself in faithfulness to an unfaithful woman as a living embodiment of God's covenantal relationship with Israel. Despite Israel's repeated unfaithfulness, God relentlessly pursued her in covenantal love.

As it turns out, each of us is also the unfaithful lover. As Gentiles, we are grafted into Israel's story because God extended Israel's covenantal promises to all who are in Christ. Yet we show just the sort of scattered unfaithfulness that this woman did to Hosea and that Israel did to God. We need just as much of God's unyielding, relentless love and mercy as Israel did.

The unfaithful woman was offered marriage to a faithful man who would provide for her. Instead she filled her life with idolatry, sin, and anxious striving for her basic provisions, securing them by dubious means. The woman sought to impress others, pursuing attention and fame. She "adorned herself with her ring and jewelry, and went after her lovers" (Hosea 2:13). She mocked her husband's fidelity by seductively parading herself throughout her town.

We find in her life an uncomfortable resonance with our own lives. We often forget that our basic provisions come not from our striving or work but from God's faithfulness. Further, we are anxious to refine our reputations, craft our brands, and become respected in our fields of work. Fame and attention are our idols, and we dress ourselves up for social media. To put it bluntly, we forget God.

Yet despite the woman's unfaithfulness, Hosea was faithful. Despite Israel's unfaithfulness, God bound himself in covenantal love. And despite our unfaithfulness, forgetfulness, and idolatry, God is relentlessly faithful.

As you pray, thank God for his faithful pursuit of you. Ask God for illumination to see your own waywardness of body, mind, and heart. Close with John Donne's prayer-poem, which evocatively captures our need for God to overcome our wayward loves.

Pray:

Batter my heart, three-person'd God, for you
As yet but knock, breathe, shine, and seek to mend;
That I may rise and stand, o'erthrow me, and bend
Your force to break, blow, burn, and make me new.
I, like an usurp'd town to another due,
Labor to admit you, but oh, to no end;
Reason, your viceroy in me, me should defend,
But is captiv'd, and proves weak or untrue.
Yet dearly I love you, and would be lov'd fain,
But am betroth'd unto your enemy;
Divorce me, untie or break that knot again,
Take me to you, imprison me, for I,
Except you enthrall me, never shall be free,
Nor ever chaste, except you ravish me. Amen.

("Batter My Heart, Three-Person'd God")

Saturday of Easter Week
FRANCIS CAPITANIO

Read: *Hosea 6:1–3*

"Come, let us return to the LORD;
    for he has torn us, that he may heal us;
    he has struck us down, and he will bind us up.
After two days he will revive us;
    on the third day he will raise us up,
    that we may live before him.
Let us know; let us press on to know the LORD;
    his going out is sure as the dawn;
he will come to us as the showers,
    as the spring rains that water the earth."

Reflect:

"Come, let us return to the LORD" (v. 1). This is the way to fulfill the first and greatest commandment: Love the Lord your God with all your heart, with all your soul, and with all your mind. To love God, we must return. To return, we must pray.

On the third day after his death, the Lord rose up from the grave. It was he, rather than Israel, who was torn to pieces. For the sake of his people, it was he who was injured, even to the point of death. But on the third day after his death—the "eighth day" of new creation—Jesus was restored, along with all of Israel, back to the fullness of the divine life promised to humankind by God the Father. Through that resurrection, Jesus the Messiah made the way for Israel and the nations to live in the presence of their God forever and find eternal peace.

That's what we tap into every time we pray. The eighth day opens the way for us into God's presence each and every day, so that we know it is there when we return to the Lord in prayer. We are eighth-day people. We return to the Lord from our lives of worry, injury, heartache, and sin. When we forget the Lord, or we get buried by the world, then we remember that we must return—we must push through and turn back to face the one who can and will revive us.

Every time we turn to behold his presence through prayer, we remember what the Lord made possible on the eighth day more than two thousand years ago. We are reminded of his promise to always be there when our hearts turn back to him.

As you pray, recall this reality, claim this promise, and be at peace.

Pray:

O Father, most merciful, who in the beginning did create us, and by the passion of your only begotten Son have created us anew, work in us now, we ask you, both to will and to do of your good pleasure. And forasmuch as we are weak, and can do no good thing of ourselves, grant us your grace and heavenly benediction, that in whatever work we engage we may do all to your honor and glory; and that, being kept from sin and daily increasing in good works, so long as we live in the body we may ever show forth some service to you; and after our departure may receive pardon of all our sins, and attain eternal life. Amen.

(Anselm)

Second Sunday of Eastertide
WILLA KANE

Read: *Psalm 34:1–14*

I will bless the LORD at all times;
    his praise shall continually be in my mouth.
My soul makes its boast in the LORD;
    let the humble hear and be glad.
Oh, magnify the LORD with me,
    and let us exalt his name together!
I sought the LORD, and he answered me
    and delivered me from all my fears.
Those who look to him are radiant,
    and their faces shall never be ashamed.
This poor man cried, and the LORD heard him
    and saved him out of all his troubles.
The angel of the LORD encamps
    around those who fear him, and delivers them.
Oh, taste and see that the LORD is good!
    Blessed is the man who takes refuge in him!
Oh, fear the LORD, you his saints,
    for those who fear him have no lack!
The young lions suffer want and hunger;
    but those who seek the LORD lack no good thing.
Come, O children, listen to me;
    I will teach you the fear of the LORD.
What man is there who desires life
    and loves many days, that he may see good?
Keep your tongue from evil
    and your lips from speaking deceit.
Turn away from evil and do good;
    seek peace and pursue it.

Reflect:

David wrote in psalm after psalm that our hearts were made for worship and our voices were designed for praise. This is especially poignant for us to remember during Eastertide as we celebrate the resurrection and power of God. In Psalm 34, David called us to join him in living, breathing, and—every chance we get—praising the God who saves.

This call is countercultural in a world dominated by negative headlines and nanosecond messaging, in a world focused on me and mine. As king of Israel, David might have expected, even demanded, adulation from his subjects. But he found another, better way. His lungs expanded with praise for the God who met him halfway. He praised the God who freed him from his fears and rescued him from enemies and desperation. He called us to join him and modeled how to worship God.

As you pray, open your mouth to taste, and open your eyes to see, the goodness of God. Run to him and be blessed. Seek beauty. Don't lie or use profanity, instead using your mouth to taste what is good. Turn your back on sin. Do good and seek peace.

When you need him, cry out to God—he listens and rescues. Are you kicked in the gut, heartbroken, in trouble? God is there every time.

The Lord himself has paid the ransom. He has bought your freedom. He will never leave you or forsake you. Praise him and thank him.

Pray:
O God, we praise you and thank you because you will rescue your servants; no one who takes refuge in you will be condemned. Amen.

Eastertide Day 9

ELIZABETH GATEWOOD

Read: *Hosea 11:1–4, 9–11*

> When Israel was a child, I loved him,
>   and out of Egypt I called my son.
> The more they were called,
>   the more they went away;
> they kept sacrificing to the Baals
>   and burning offerings to idols.
> Yet it was I who taught Ephraim to walk;
>   I took them up by their arms,
>   but they did not know that I healed them.
> I led them with cords of kindness,
>   with the bands of love,
> and I became to them as one who eases the yoke on their jaws,
>   and I bent down to them and fed them....
> I will not execute my burning anger;
>   I will not again destroy Ephraim;
> for I am God and not a man,
>   the Holy One in your midst,
>   and I will not come in wrath.
> They shall go after the LORD;
>   he will roar like a lion;
> when he roars,
>   his children shall come trembling from the west;
> they shall come trembling like birds from Egypt,
>   and like doves from the land of Assyria,
>   and I will return them to their homes, declares the LORD.

Reflect:

We might say that parenting is a thankless job, but perhaps a more fitting description is that it is a hidden job. Each day parents provide tender and thoughtful care in a thousand small and unnoticed ways. We ensure there is milk in the fridge for morning cereal. We put towels out so they're ready after a bath. We collect discarded toys so they're not broken or lost. We schedule visits to the doctors and dentist. These small services supply the loving care that allows a child to flourish.

In Hosea 11, God was the parent and Israel the child. God had tenderly cared for Israel. He called Israel out of Egypt—a rescue from bondage that prefigured the infant Christ's sojourn to seek protection in Egypt. He taught Israel to walk. He gave Israel laws for their flourishing and protection—cords of kindness and bands of love.

Israel was the child who neither noticed God nor thanked him for his provision and nurture. Israel was the child who was bent on turning away from God.

Yet the mercy and love of God crested like waves, overcoming his anger. He simply could not punish or abandon Israel as they deserved. His love poured forth in a roar of righteousness, love, anger, and invitation all at once, a roar that is familiar to any "mama bear" who fiercely loves her children.

God will not allow the destructive bent of his children to be the final word. He will bring them home and redeem them. He will be faithful even when his children are not.

As you pray, consider the places where you are tempted to keep score and give up loving. Ask for God's mighty power to wash over you so that you might participate in his relentless love. Consider the places where you feel beyond the reach of the greatness of God's love. Imagine his love overpowering you and surrounding you.

Pray:

God, thank you for your hidden love. You have sustained us in a thousand invisible ways. We thank you for life and breath, for the blessings of family and friends, and for the sustenance and shelter that you have provided. Thank you also for your relentless pursuit of us. We confess that we are wayward and capricious children, bent on the idolatry that leads to destruction. We doubt that we are worth your time and attention. Help us to rest in our belovedness. Amen.

Eastertide Day 10

ELIZABETH GATEWOOD

Read: *Hosea 14:1–7*

> Return, O Israel, to the LORD your God,
>> for you have stumbled because of your iniquity.
> Take with you words
>> and return to the LORD;
> say to him,
>> "Take away all iniquity;
> accept what is good,
>> and we will pay with bulls
>> the vows of our lips.
> Assyria shall not save us;
>> we will not ride on horses;
> and we will say no more, 'Our God,'
>> to the work of our hands.
> In you the orphan finds mercy."
> I will heal their apostasy;
>> I will love them freely,
>> for my anger has turned from them.
> I will be like the dew to Israel;
>> he shall blossom like the lily;
>> he shall take root like the trees of Lebanon;
> his shoots shall spread out;
>> his beauty shall be like the olive,
>> and his fragrance like Lebanon.
> They shall return and dwell beneath my shadow;
>> they shall flourish like the grain;
> they shall blossom like the vine;
>> their fame shall be like the wine of Lebanon.

Reflect:

God's love and mercy have the last word. Hosea didn't mince words about the depth or severity of Israel's sin. He didn't blunt the force or power of God's anger. Yet the book of Hosea ends on a hopeful note with God's promise to heal and bless. In chapter 14, we have a prayer and a vision. Both are instructive for us.

First, God gave his people a prayer to pray: "Take with you words" in your return to the Lord (v. 2). Hosea knew that sometimes we grasp for language, not sure what we should ask of God. In this prayer, the people were taught to ask for his forgiveness and instructed to name their idols, the foreign powers and the gods they had made and that they trusted.

Second, God gave his people a vision. Hosea mentioned six different plants in this chapter: the lily, the cedar of Lebanon, the olive tree, grain, a grapevine, and a juniper. Israel would again flourish as these plants do, offering fragrant beauty, shade, and nourishment. The grace of God would saturate them like dew.

Call to your mind what spring is like as it renews our sense of the goodness of God. Purple coneflowers are lush in their green leaves. Fragile columbine flowers bloom. The naked limbs of trees morph into the shelter of new oak, maple, and dogwood leaves. The shy smell of nicotiana flowers fills the air. Zinnias and sunflowers offer summer color. Gardens flourish and herbs abound.

What if we were to see the lush abundance of this blooming as an image of God's present and future work in us? God's dew will rest on us, and we will flourish as these plants do in the glorious summer months.

As you pray, follow the structure of Hosea's prayer: confession and a plea for forgiveness, naming of idols, and proclamation of God's faithfulness. Imagine God's dew of grace resting on you and bringing fruitfulness and healing to your life.

Pray:

God, it's unimaginable that we who are so wayward and forgetful, so idolatrous and doubtful, should flourish. Forgive us our sins. Forgive us for trusting in the creations of our hands and minds to fulfill us or save us. We long to be fruitful, healthy, and whole. We marvel at your faithfulness and your commitment to us. Soak us with the dew of your grace and renew your life in us. Amen.

Eastertide Day 11
ELIZABETH GATEWOOD

Read: *Ephesians 1:3–14*

Blessed be the God and Father of our Lord Jesus Christ, who has blessed us in Christ with every spiritual blessing in the heavenly places, even as he chose us in him before the foundation of the world, that we should be holy and blameless before him. In love he predestined us for adoption to himself as sons through Jesus Christ, according to the purpose of his will, to the praise of his glorious grace, with which he has blessed us in the Beloved. In him we have redemption through his blood, the forgiveness of our trespasses, according to the riches of his grace, which he lavished upon us, in all wisdom and insight making known to us the mystery of his will, according to his purpose, which he set forth in Christ as a plan for the fullness of time, to unite all things in him, things in heaven and things on earth.

In him we have obtained an inheritance, having been predestined according to the purpose of him who works all things according to the counsel of his will, so that we who were the first to hope in Christ might be to the praise of his glory. In him you also, when you heard the word of truth, the gospel of your salvation, and believed in him, were sealed with the promised Holy Spirit, who is the guarantee of our inheritance until we acquire possession of it, to the praise of his glory.

Reflect:

The beginning of Paul's letter to the Ephesians reads like a child excitedly recounting the gifts received on Christmas morning. It feels like what would spill out of a child's mouth on this most hallowed day of gift giving. "And then I got this, and then I got this! And then I got this and this and—oh wait, I forgot to tell you about this!"

Paul had hardly gotten past his greeting to the church at Ephesus before he poured forth with a story of who God is, what God has given us, and who we are in Christ.

What would it look like to be so rooted in God's story and so saturated in thankfulness that we simply could not help joyfully recounting a list of all the rich blessings that God has given us?

Too often we forget. We are distracted by our current ailments, however legitimate, by the confining boundaries of a particular situation, the pain of a failing relationship, or the longing for a child, a new job, a path out of depression, or a friend. We come to God not with joyful remembrance but with tired, and sometimes faithless and cynical, prayers.

But Paul brought us back to God's big story. And here is what is gloriously true for those of us who are in Christ. We are

- blessed with every spiritual blessing in Christ;
- chosen before the creation of the world;
- predestined for adoption to sonship as God's children;
- freely lavished with grace;
- forgiven of our sins;
- redeemed by God's blood; and
- marked with the seal of the Holy Spirit.

Perhaps this seems real to you today. Perhaps it doesn't. Or perhaps, even if it is real, it seems irrelevant to your actual problems. As you pray, consider this list. Which gift stirs you? Which leaves you with questions? Which do you struggle to believe God has given you? Which do you simply forget?

Pray:

Pray aloud the words from Ephesians 1:3–14, substituting *I* or *me* for *we* and *us*, respectively. Rejoice in what Christ has done for you.

Eastertide Day 12

ELIZABETH GATEWOOD

Read: *Ephesians 1:15–23*

For this reason, because I have heard of your faith in the Lord Jesus
and your love toward all the saints, I do not cease to give thanks
for you, remembering you in my prayers, that the God of our Lord
Jesus Christ, the Father of glory, may give you the Spirit of wisdom
and of revelation in the knowledge of him, having the eyes of your
hearts enlightened, that you may know what is the hope to which he
has called you, what are the riches of his glorious inheritance in the
saints, and what is the immeasurable greatness of his power toward
us who believe, according to the working of his great might that
he worked in Christ when he raised him from the dead and seated
him at his right hand in the heavenly places, far above all rule and
authority and power and dominion, and above every name that is
named, not only in this age but also in the one to come. And he put
all things under his feet and gave him as head over all things to the
church, which is his body, the fullness of him who fills all in all.

Reflect:

There are certain factions of Christianity that have envisioned God as
muscular, victorious, conquering. Some have wielded the name of Jesus as
a weapon to accomplish their own ends and maintained an over-realized
expectation of what God would choose to accomplish in certain present
circumstances, be they political, financial, or otherwise.

But there are also others that have so domesticated God that they hardly
expect anything of him. God is reduced to a flat figure in our "moralistic
therapeutic deism," a vague and only vaguely comforting figure in our spiritual imaginations.

We see something quite different in Ephesians.

God has worked his power to raise Jesus from the dead and seat him
at the right hand of the Father in the heavenly realms. Jesus is established
as ruler of all times and places. Catch the wild part: This same power of

"immeasurable greatness" (v. 19) is at work in us who believe in Jesus. This is not a power that we can wield for our own ends. It's also not a power that we can domesticate or deny. God's power is power itself. And this power is at work in you. This power is at work in me.

God's power isn't only or primarily at work when we feel holy: at church, or when doing something explicitly Christian such as tithing, feeding the poor, sharing the gospel, or disciplining our children. This power is at work in our ordinary lives—at the kitchen sink, on the webcam, and on the T-ball field. God's Spirit indwells us and his power is in us—made perfect, in fact, in our very weakness.

As you pray, consider whether you tend toward claiming God's power for your own ends or denying and forgetting that God is powerful. Ask God to reveal his power and presence in the midst of your ordinary life.

Pray:

God, we are surprised that you would show up in the midst of our ordinary lives. How incredible it is that your power is at work in us, the same power that raised Jesus from the dead! It feels too great, Lord, like a wind that is too strong. We aren't sure we believe that, and if it's true, we aren't sure what to do with it. Remind us that your power is never absent from your love. Remind us that your Holy Spirit enfolds us, empowers us, and indwells us. Give us a strong assurance of your power and presence. Let us submit to this power and to your loving embrace. Amen.

Eastertide Day 13
WILLA KANE

Read: *Ephesians 2:1–10*

And you were dead in the trespasses and sins in which you once walked, following the course of this world, following the prince of the power of the air, the spirit that is now at work in the sons of disobedience—among whom we all once lived in the passions of our flesh, carrying out the desires of the body and the mind, and were by nature children of wrath, like the rest of mankind. But God, being rich in mercy, because of the great love with which he loved us, even when we were dead in our trespasses, made us alive together with Christ—by grace you have been saved—and raised us up with him and seated us with him in the heavenly places in Christ Jesus, so that in the coming ages he might show the immeasurable riches of his grace in kindness toward us in Christ Jesus. For by grace you have been saved through faith. And this is not your own doing; it is the gift of God, not a result of works, so that no one may boast. For we are his workmanship, created in Christ Jesus for good works, which God prepared beforehand, that we should walk in them.

Reflect:

When visiting the doctor's office, we dread a dire medical diagnosis. Here in his letter to the Ephesians, Paul delivered a different sort of diagnosis, one even more dire: "dead in the trespasses and sins."

We were spiritually dead and separated from the God who made us, unable to escape the many consequences of our sins.

In the face of such hopelessness, what could possibly happen?

"*But God*" (v. 4, emphasis added). These words have been called the most beautiful words in the Bible—our gospel prescription in two little words.

But God. But God stepped in. But God intervened. But God came after us. But God drew near to spiritually dead people and, because he loved us, made us alive together with Christ.

These two words are the pivot point that mark the moment at which everything changed. We were flatlined on the operating table, our hearts choked in spiritual death. But God, in his mercy and kindness, performed a complete heart transplant. We were hopeless, helpless, and alone. But God, rich in mercy, made us alive together with Christ!

As you pray, settle into these two words: "But God." Let them fill your mind, heart, and soul. Challenge the hardships you face with these words. Thank God for his great love for us, for his extravagant mercy, for the gift of kindness that promises us immeasurable riches in Christ. If our God has done all these things, how much more can we count on him to be with us in the night, during days that are hard, and on into eternity?

Pray:

Dear Lord and Savior Jesus Christ: I hold all my weakness to your strength, my failure to your faithfulness, my sinfulness to your perfection, my loneliness to your compassion, my little pains to your great agony on the Cross. I pray that you will cleanse me, strengthen me, guide me, so that in all ways my life may be lived as you would have it lived, without cowardice and for you alone. Show me how to live in true humility, true contrition, and true love. Amen.

(Anglican Church in North America Book of Common Prayer)

Eastertide Day 14
WILLA KANE

Read: *Ephesians 2:12–17*

Remember that you were at that time separated from Christ,
alienated from the commonwealth of Israel and strangers to the
covenants of promise, having no hope and without God in the
world. But now in Christ Jesus you who once were far off have been
brought near by the blood of Christ. For he himself is our peace,
who has made us both one and has broken down in his flesh the
dividing wall of hostility by abolishing the law of commandments
expressed in ordinances, that he might create in himself one new
man in place of the two, so making peace, and might reconcile us
both to God in one body through the cross, thereby killing the
hostility. And he came and preached peace to you who were far off
and peace to those who were near.

Reflect:

Paul loved to highlight the difference that Christ makes in our lives. Just a
few verses earlier, he recalled how things used to be and rejoiced in how they
are. Yes, we were dead in sin. But God is rich in mercy, and out of his great
love, he has made us alive in Christ.

Paul began with another impossible situation: the messy, insurmount-
able interpersonal divisions in our lives. "The dividing wall of hostility" (v.
14) is such an appropriate image for how it feels to be separated from another
person. When you are in conflict with other people or divided by a vast array
of differences, you may feel that the problem is impossible to overcome.

But the good news is that God has overcome for us. God himself has
demolished the dividing wall of hostility. Jesus himself is our peace, even
when all hope for reconciliation seems lost. Loving other people well is not
just up to us. It's not even possible on our own. If we are in Christ, the walls
that divide us have been torn down, and love pours out.

As you pray, pause and take some time to look at your life with ruthless honesty. What relationships in your life need to be restored? Where is love in short supply? Where do walls still exist? Blessedly, there is a remedy. Open your heart to God in confession and come to the cross where love and mercy meet, where the love of Jesus pours down and out. Ask the one who has paid the price and made the way for your own reconciliation to pour out love and forgiveness through you.

Pray:

O Lord, you have met me in mercy and love. You have not dealt with me as my sins deserve. As Jesus hung on the cross, he offered forgiveness to those who had not even asked for it. Help me to forgive the one I hold a grudge against. Teach me to love freely and generously. Thank you for the love of Jesus, which you long to pour into me and through me. Amen.

Third Sunday of Easter
BRANDON WALSH

Read: *Psalm 46*

> God is our refuge and strength,
>> a very present help in trouble.
> Therefore we will not fear though the earth gives way,
>> though the mountains be moved into the heart of the sea,
> though its waters roar and foam,
>> though the mountains tremble at its swelling.   *Selah*
> There is a river whose streams make glad the city of God,
>> the holy habitation of the Most High.
> God is in the midst of her; she shall not be moved;
>> God will help her when morning dawns.
> The nations rage, the kingdoms totter;
>> he utters his voice, the earth melts.
> The LORD of hosts is with us;
>> the God of Jacob is our fortress.   *Selah*
> Come, behold the works of the LORD,
>> how he has brought desolations on the earth.
> He makes wars cease to the end of the earth;
>> he breaks the bow and shatters the spear;
>> he burns the chariots with fire.
> "Be still, and know that I am God.
>> I will be exalted among the nations,
>> I will be exalted in the earth!"
> The LORD of hosts is with us;
>> the God of Jacob is our fortress.   *Selah*

Reflect:

"Be still." These are words that every parent knows all too well! Small children fidget, squirm, and make noise all the time. Knees bounce under the table, fingers tap on car windows, and chairs rock back and forth at just the moment when the noise is most noticeable.

We are not so different from our children. Sure, at some point we learn a bit of impulse control. We stop fidgeting quite so much, or we develop quieter and less distracting ways to do it. All the while, beneath a more presentable exterior we are squirming on the inside. Our brains flit from thing to thing, looking for distraction. Our smartphones throw gasoline on this fire. But though the distraction of technology may make our restlessness worse, in truth, our nervous anxiety comes from a deeper root.

In Psalm 46:10, the Lord beckons us, "Be still, and know that I am God."

Be. Still. This psalm paints a picture of the world in tumult. It is a world giving way to chaos, to uncreation, where the mountains are thrown into the very heart of the sea. Mountains are firm and reliable; the sea is capricious and strange. When mountains are hurled into the sea, things have gone awry. But even in moments when the world seems chaotic and unreliable, we can find our full refuge in God.

When the waves crash and the earth shakes, when pandemic isolates and politics divide, we must be still, to turn away from the taunting voices of distraction and hysteria, and to return to the living waters of God. Only in such a place will the fidgeting of our souls find its rest.

That peace is offered today as well, the psalmist reassured us. As you pray, practice living in the invitation of this psalm. Be still. Be still and know that the Lord is God. In him all things hold together and find their completion. If you belong to Jesus, the Spirit will make rivers of living water flow through your heart.

Pray:

Almighty Father, make us still—still enough to feel your breath on our faces and in our lungs; still enough to tame the raging waters within us and around us; still enough to know you even as we are fully known by you. From the throne of your Son, true waters flow into your people by your Holy Spirit. May we be still enough to drink, still enough to bear fruit in every season; in the name of Jesus. Amen.

Eastertide Day 16

ELIZABETH GATEWOOD

Read: *Ephesians 3:1–13*

For this reason I, Paul, a prisoner of Christ Jesus on behalf of you Gentiles—assuming that you have heard of the stewardship of God's grace that was given to me for you, how the mystery was made known to me by revelation, as I have written briefly. When you read this, you can perceive my insight into the mystery of Christ, which was not made known to the sons of men in other generations as it has now been revealed to his holy apostles and prophets by the Spirit. This mystery is that the Gentiles are fellow heirs, members of the same body, and partakers of the promise in Christ Jesus through the gospel.

Of this gospel I was made a minister according to the gift of God's grace, which was given me by the working of his power. To me, though I am the very least of all the saints, this grace was given, to preach to the Gentiles the unsearchable riches of Christ, and to bring to light for everyone what is the plan of the mystery hidden for ages in God, who created all things, so that through the church the manifold wisdom of God might now be made known to the rulers and authorities in the heavenly places. This was according to the eternal purpose that he has realized in Christ Jesus our Lord, in whom we have boldness and access with confidence through our faith in him. So I ask you not to lose heart over what I am suffering for you, which is your glory.

Reflect:

Paul had a clarity about his story and his vocation: He was given a particular grace and revelation from God. His particular vocation was to preach the gospel to the Gentiles, telling them that they were included in God's kingdom and also sharing about the boundless riches of Christ with them.

Paul saw himself as a messenger and participant in God's big story. He spilled over with excitement as he described that story in Ephesians 1, and he simply gave the footnotes in Ephesians 3:9–12.

It might seem obvious that Paul had a clear calling and a place within God's big story. After all, Paul was a colossal figure in the early church. Perhaps it's a harder leap for us to believe that God has given each of us a particular vocation and a particular place within God's story. Our lives feel ordinary, full of struggle, insignificant, pragmatically driven, speckled with failure, and punctured by suffering.

Yet Paul was very much like us. He persisted in doing his work even though he felt unworthy to do it. He persisted in doing his work even though his work caused him to suffer.

What might we learn from looking to Paul as an ordinary person? He was a sinner who struggled and suffered his way through ministry. Yet he persisted in courageously and energetically doing the task that God had called him to do.

As you pray, consider what call God has placed on your life. Pray that God might clarify his will and encourage you in your vocation, regardless of what occupation happens to be yours at the moment. Meditate on Paul's story, his sufferings, and his courage.

Pray:

Heavenly Father, it is difficult for us to believe you have called us and equipped us. We feel so ordinary, and our days are filled with ordinary things: diapers and emails, carpool lines and meetings, paperwork and chores. Have you truly called each of us with a specific vocation and given us a particular role in your big story? We ask that we might be encouraged by Paul's story. Equip us in the midst of our ordinary days to bring glory to you. Clarify that to which you have called each of us. And give us courage to persist in the midst of self-doubt, suffering, and failure; in the name of your Son, Jesus Christ. Amen.

Eastertide Day 17
ELIZABETH GATEWOOD

Read: *Ephesians 3:14–21*

For this reason I bow my knees before the Father, from whom every family in heaven and on earth is named, that according to the riches of his glory he may grant you to be strengthened with power through his Spirit in your inner being, so that Christ may dwell in your hearts through faith—that you, being rooted and grounded in love, may have strength to comprehend with all the saints what is the breadth and length and height and depth, and to know the love of Christ that surpasses knowledge, that you may be filled with all the fullness of God.

Now to him who is able to do far more abundantly than all that we ask or think, according to the power at work within us, to him be glory in the church and in Christ Jesus throughout all generations, forever and ever. Amen.

Reflect:

As Paul prayed for the Ephesians in chapter 3, he made three references to God's power.

First, he prayed that God's power would strengthen them so that Christ might dwell in their hearts through faith. Though this isn't a theological treatise on faith and free will, this passage suggests that faith in Christ is a joint effort between the animating power of the Holy Spirit and an individual's will.

Second, Paul prayed that the Ephesians would have the power to grasp the love of Christ. This is a love that is higher, wider, and deeper than they could imagine. And this is a love that surpasses knowledge. Paul spilt over with joy and excitement about the love of God. He deeply desired for this budding church at Ephesus to grasp this love as fundamental to the gospel.

Third, Paul referenced God's power that is at work within us. He had made this point already in Ephesians 1: The same power that raised Jesus from the dead is at work in those who are in Christ. The astonishing reality is that we are animated by the same force that conquered death.

God is power! But God's power is worked out in love. It is not a power marked by greed, selfish gain, or self-centeredness. God's power is marked by love. It takes the shape of the cross. It moves in the illuminating and empowering wind of the Holy Spirit.

As you pray, consider that the most powerful thing in the entire world is a power that is love-shaped. It is a power that moves toward you and me in self-sacrificial love and embrace. It is a power that brings life.

Pray:

Lord, I cast myself before you. O spurn me not from you, unworthy though I am of all your wonderful goodness. O grant me more and more of humility, and love, and faith, and hope, and longing for a complete renewal into your image. Lord, help me and hear me. I come to you as my only Savior. O be you my help, my strength, my peace, and joy, and consolation; my Alpha and Omega, my all in all. Amen.

(William Wilberforce)

Eastertide Day 18

GAYLE HEASLIP

Read: *Ephesians 4:1–7, 11–16*

I therefore, a prisoner for the Lord, urge you to walk in a manner worthy of the calling to which you have been called, with all humility and gentleness, with patience, bearing with one another in love, eager to maintain the unity of the Spirit in the bond of peace. There is one body and one Spirit—just as you were called to the one hope that belongs to your call—one Lord, one faith, one baptism, one God and Father of all, who is over all and through all and in all. But grace was given to each one of us according to the measure of Christ's gift....

And he gave the apostles, the prophets, the evangelists, the shepherds and teachers, to equip the saints for the work of ministry, for building up the body of Christ, until we all attain to the unity of the faith and of the knowledge of the Son of God, to mature manhood, to the measure of the stature of the fullness of Christ, so that we may no longer be children, tossed to and fro by the waves and carried about by every wind of doctrine, by human cunning, by craftiness in deceitful schemes. Rather, speaking the truth in love, we are to grow up in every way into him who is the head, into Christ, from whom the whole body, joined and held together by every joint with which it is equipped, when each part is working properly, makes the body grow so that it builds itself up in love.

Reflect:

Looking at the world around us, and often the one within us, we see division and fragmentation. Our longing for wholeness is challenged by such brokenness. As we sit among the fragments of shattered dreams, do we dare to envision the healing presence of God's kingdom as a growing reality?

Our God has promised to bring what is broken into a singular wholeness and unity through Christ. We are mended through the one faith and one baptism into a oneness with the one God and Father of all. His is the unifying power; his is the mending love.

In his wisdom, the Lord has generously equipped his saints for their ministry in our wounded world. By his mercy, we are built up and grown in love so that we might reflect, even in the midst of brokenness, the wholeness of the one who joins us and holds all things together.

As we grow in the knowledge of the person of Christ, and as each of us inhabits our roles for the sake of others, the church grows into a fullness none of us can achieve alone. This growth happens slowly through a Spirit-led transformation.

As you prepare to pray, pause and consider what is going on in your own heart. What do you imagine wholeness to look like in Christ's body on earth? Will you trust the Lord to mend brokenness, heal wounds, and bring unity? Will you give yourself to his process to do so and live into your own maturity under the Spirit's tender and powerful leading? Will you do this in community?

Pray:

Lord, may I be content with my place in your body on earth. May I be willing to lean on others for the support given by my brothers and sisters in the grace, love, and wisdom supplied by your overseeing love. May I boldly embrace the unifying, maturing work of the Spirit to bring us all into the whole measure of the fullness of Christ. Amen.

Eastertide Day 19

GAYLE HEASLIP

Read: *Ephesians 4:17–32*

Now this I say and testify in the Lord, that you must no longer walk as the Gentiles do, in the futility of their minds. They are darkened in their understanding, alienated from the life of God because of the ignorance that is in them, due to their hardness of heart. They have become callous and have given themselves up to sensuality, greedy to practice every kind of impurity. But that is not the way you learned Christ!—assuming that you have heard about him and were taught in him, as the truth is in Jesus, to put off your old self, which belongs to your former manner of life and is corrupt through deceitful desires, and to be renewed in the spirit of your minds, and to put on the new self, created after the likeness of God in true righteousness and holiness.

Therefore, having put away falsehood, let each one of you speak the truth with his neighbor, for we are members one of another. Be angry and do not sin; do not let the sun go down on your anger, and give no opportunity to the devil. Let the thief no longer steal, but rather let him labor, doing honest work with his own hands, so that he may have something to share with anyone in need. Let no corrupting talk come out of your mouths, but only such as is good for building up, as fits the occasion, that it may give grace to those who hear. And do not grieve the Holy Spirit of God, by whom you were sealed for the day of redemption. Let all bitterness and wrath and anger and clamor and slander be put away from you, along with all malice. Be kind to one another, tenderhearted, forgiving one another, as God in Christ forgave you.

Reflect:

"God is light, and in him is no darkness at all," John proclaimed in 1 John 1:5. Paul urged us in this passage from Ephesians to live as children of light, to be a mirror reflecting and a window revealing God our Father.

Living as children of the light means that we choose our way forward each day, always opening our hearts to the Lord. If we harden our hearts to him, we lose sensitivity to his presence and leading; our understanding becomes increasingly darkened until we become separated from the life of God.

Instead, we put off the old self of our darkened minds and put on the new self in Christ. In Christ there is abundant light, light that clarifies to us what true righteousness and holiness looks like as we gaze on him whose life is the light shining in the darkness. We want to live continually in this bright new life that is his gift to us.

How difficult such daily choices can be, however. How easy to tear down others with our words; to hold bitterness, anger, and hatred in our hearts; and to grieve the Holy Spirit. How easy to be self-centered instead of speaking to build others up and working with the intent to share with those in need.

Where do you find yourself in darkness today, separated from the light? What relationship cries out for the light of Christ's upbuilding love through your words, your generosity, and the kindness and compassion that flow from a light-drenched heart? What prayer rises up from within you, beloved of God, for his light in place of darkness?

Pray that you will respond to God's invitation to live as a child of the light.

Pray:

Lord, you know the places within me that lean toward darkness. How I long for your light to fill me! As I come before you now, I freely choose to put off the old self and live in the light of your holy presence. Strengthen me in each choice to choose again and again from a heart and mind surrendered to the light of your love. In so doing, may I discover flowing from me the loving words and actions that reveal you, Father of light. Amen.

Eastertide Day 20
GAYLE HEASLIP

Read: *Ephesians 5:1–4, 15–21*

Therefore be imitators of God, as beloved children. And walk in love, as Christ loved us and gave himself up for us, a fragrant offering and sacrifice to God.

But sexual immorality and all impurity or covetousness must not even be named among you, as is proper among saints. Let there be no filthiness nor foolish talk nor crude joking, which are out of place, but instead let there be thanksgiving....

Look carefully then how you walk, not as unwise but as wise, making the best use of the time, because the days are evil. Therefore do not be foolish, but understand what the will of the Lord is. And do not get drunk with wine, for that is debauchery, but be filled with the Spirit, addressing one another in psalms and hymns and spiritual songs, singing and making melody to the Lord with your heart, giving thanks always and for everything to God the Father in the name of our Lord Jesus Christ, submitting to one another out of reverence for Christ.

Reflect:

Imagine a landscape drenched in an early-morning sunshine that illuminates every meadow flower, every dew-kissed blade of grass. As you step into this sunny field, your fingertips graze the soft tips of new growth reaching for the light. Lifting your face to the sky, you stop and close your eyes, receiving a deep sense of warmth and well-being.

Such is the inheritance of God's beloved. Once, we lived in darkness, bereft of light. Our hands groped before us, seeking a way forward. Our feet stumbled, seeking stability. Our minds were darkened and fearful. Now we are light and walk as children of the light in Christ, full of glory. Our hearts are illuminated, and our minds are cleared by this truth: He is, and we are his. We drink in this truth and taste its bright goodness and lingering satisfaction.

Where else but in this bright landscape would we long to dwell? What other path but this path of goodness and truth could satisfy us? As we embrace these desires from the inmost places of our hearts, we will discover, in the Lord's responsive affection for us, what pleases him, and we will come to understand what his will is for us so that we might follow this light always.

As you pray, ask the Lord to fill you with longing for his goodness and truth.

Pray:

O you high and holy One that inhabits eternity, you are to be feared and loved by all your servants. All your works praise you, O God; and we especially give thanks unto you for your marvelous love in Christ Jesus, by whom you have reconciled the world to yourself. You have given us exceeding great and precious promises. You have sealed them with his blood. You have confirmed them by his resurrection and ascension, and the coming of the Holy Spirit. We thank you that you have given us so many happy opportunities of knowing the truth as it is in Jesus, even the mystery which was hid from ages and generations, but is now revealed to them that believe. Amen.

(John Wesley)

Eastertide Day 21

GAYLE HEASLIP

Read: *Ephesians 6:1–12*

Children, obey your parents in the Lord, for this is right. "Honor
your father and mother" (this is the first commandment with a
promise), "that it may go well with you and that you may live long
in the land." Fathers, do not provoke your children to anger, but
bring them up in the discipline and instruction of the Lord.

Bondservants, obey your earthly masters with fear and trem-
bling, with a sincere heart, as you would Christ, not by the way
of eye-service, as people-pleasers, but as bondservants of Christ,
doing the will of God from the heart, rendering service with a good
will as to the Lord and not to man, knowing that whatever good
anyone does, this he will receive back from the Lord, whether he is a
bondservant or is free. Masters, do the same to them, and stop your
threatening, knowing that he who is both their Master and yours is
in heaven, and that there is no partiality with him.

Finally, be strong in the Lord and in the strength of his might.
Put on the whole armor of God, that you may be able to stand
against the schemes of the devil. For we do not wrestle against flesh
and blood, but against the rulers, against the authorities, against the
cosmic powers over this present darkness, against the spiritual forces
of evil in the heavenly places.

Reflect:

All is held in God's gaze, and all of the Lord's desires are rooted in his nature
to love. Though there is surely a great power differential between the Lord
and his people, he relates to us only in love and exercises his authority for
the sake of love. When we realize that all relationships—whether they are
between children and parents, husbands and wives, or servants and masters—
are also held within his loving desires for us, we see them in a fresh way.

The knotted tensions of power within relationships can be loosened when
we choose to follow the Lord's command to love others. When we yoke our

lives to his, we are invited to live in freedom and to think of others as fellow children of God. What is more, the Lord promises that he will reward us for whatever good is done, no matter our position. Such choosing does not come easily, and daily living in this choice requires strength beyond us, a power born of the Spirit. Be strong *in the Lord* and in *his* mighty power.

To do this, we put on spiritual armor given to us through dependence on him. Then we can stand against the schemes of unseen spiritual evil and the machinations of a world that values utility above honor. In his strength we can resist the external forces that frame relationships by power alone so that we are free to love in giving, not grabbing. In this we will bear witness to the Lord's overcoming love.

Pray that you will learn to love as God loves.

Pray:

O merciful God, fill our hearts, we pray you, with the graces of your Holy Spirit, with love, joy, peace, longsuffering, gentleness, goodness, faith, meekness, temperance. Teach us to love those who hate us; to pray for those who despitefully use us; that we may be the children of you, our Father, who makes your sun to shine on the evil and on the good, and sends rain on the just and the unjust. Amen.

(Anselm)

Fourth Sunday of Easter

MADISON PERRY

Read: *Psalm 20*

> May the LORD answer you in the day of trouble!
>> May the name of the God of Jacob protect you!
> May he send you help from the sanctuary
>> and give you support from Zion!
> May he remember all your offerings
>> and regard with favor your burnt sacrifices!   *Selah*
> May he grant you your heart's desire
>> and fulfill all your plans!
> May we shout for joy over your salvation,
>> and in the name of our God set up our banners!
> May the LORD fulfill all your petitions!
> Now I know that the LORD saves his anointed;
>> he will answer him from his holy heaven
>> with the saving might of his right hand.
> Some trust in chariots and some in horses,
>> but we trust in the name of the LORD our God.
> They collapse and fall,
>> but we rise and stand upright.
> O LORD, save the king!
>> May he answer us when we call.

Reflect:

This is the prayer of a people at war who are united behind their king. It was sung on the day of battle, beginning with those who stood with King David. Today, we pray this with our eyes fixed on the Lord's Anointed One, Jesus Christ. Jesus is the focal point of the action in heaven and on earth, his battle against evil the most important conflict. When we pray, "Now I know that the LORD saves his anointed" (v. 6), we understand that the resurrection is the best evidence that the Lord saves Christ.

Consider this: "May [God] grant you your heart's desire and fulfill all your plans!" (v. 4). If you were to read this out of context, no doubt you would take it differently. But in context, this verse doesn't refer to *our* desires, but to those of our King. Jesus similarly taught his disciples to pray, "Your kingdom come, your will be done, on earth as it is in heaven" (Matthew 6:10).

How would it feel to pray this way? Our responses vary, ranging from fear at our loss of control to sweet relief at no longer having to pretend to be a ruler. Do you resist praying this psalm? Or is it like a song drifting to you from a land you long to visit and dwell in forever, the land where Christ rules?

Begin your time of prayer by worshipping God: Father, Son, and Holy Spirit. Call on the Lord for victory in your own battles and ask that our Lord's kingdom would come. Plead for God's will to be done in your life. Close your time with Martin Luther's beautiful hymn.

Pray:

A mighty fortress is our God, a bulwark never failing;
Our Helper He, amid the flood of mortal ills prevailing;
For still our ancient foe doth seek to work us woe;
His craft and pow'r are great, and, armed with cruel hate,
On earth is not his equal.
And though this world, with devils filled, should threaten to undo us,
We will not fear, for God hath willed His truth to triumph through us.
The Prince of Darkness grim, we tremble not for him;
His rage we can endure, for lo, his doom is sure;
One little word shall fell him.
That word above all earthly pow'rs no thanks to them abideth;
The Spirit and the gifts are ours through Him who with us sideth.
Let goods and kindred go, this mortal life also,
The body they may kill; God's truth abideth still;
His kingdom is forever! Amen.

("A Mighty Fortress Is Our God")

Eastertide Day 23
SALLY BREEDLOVE

Read: *Ephesians 6:13–20*

Therefore take up the whole armor of God, that you may be able to withstand in the evil day, and having done all, to stand firm. Stand therefore, having fastened on the belt of truth, and having put on the breastplate of righteousness, and, as shoes for your feet, having put on the readiness given by the gospel of peace. In all circumstances take up the shield of faith, with which you can extinguish all the flaming darts of the evil one; and take the helmet of salvation, and the sword of the Spirit, which is the word of God, praying at all times in the Spirit, with all prayer and supplication. To that end, keep alert with all perseverance, making supplication for all the saints, and also for me, that words may be given to me in opening my mouth boldly to proclaim the mystery of the gospel, for which I am an ambassador in chains, that I may declare it boldly, as I ought to speak.

Reflect:

Paul wrote these words from prison. His circumstances urge us to ask: Can good come out of being severely restricted? Can imprisonment be turned to blessing?

The Bible assures us it can be so. Joseph did excellent work for each person who kept him in bondage: the rich Potiphar, the head jailer, and even Pharaoh himself. The exiled Moses learned how to live in the desert and gained shepherding skills as he served his father-in-law for forty years as a herdsman. Daniel never got to go home; he spent his life at the beck and call of foreign kings. Jesus said no man ever born was greater than John the Baptist, but John's exit from prison was his beheading. Paul wrote much of the New Testament while in shackles.

How is the Spirit calling you to receive the restrictions that shape your own life right now? How is he inviting you to see your minutes and hours as a gift?

Any distress or restriction we face does not have to undo us. It can make us more deeply human if we let it. Paul urged us to let truth, righteousness, peace, faith, and salvation shape our lives. He reminded us that the Scriptures and prayer give us the strength we need.

Ponder Paul's words here in Ephesians. How does God want to grow you so that you become stronger and wiser? How is he inviting you into new rhythms of loving and living?

Pray for yourself. Pray you will steward your time well. Pray you will embrace new disciplines for your life with God. Pray you will enter into new ways of being at rest. Pray you will see the opportunities already waiting for you to love and to serve.

Pray:

O Lord, I pray to you, alongside brothers and sisters around the globe. All good things come from you. Please pour into us truth, righteousness, peace, and salvation. Wake us all up to our sin and inadequacies. Open our lips so that we may praise you and pray for others. Please let the world know of your salvation. Fill the hungry; comfort the brokenhearted; and give rest to the weary. May you be praised in all things and at all times now and everywhere, our Rock and our Redeemer. Amen.

Eastertide Day 24
KARI WEST

Read: *Philippians 1:3–11*

> I thank my God in all my remembrance of you, always in every prayer of mine for you all making my prayer with joy, because of your partnership in the gospel from the first day until now. And I am sure of this, that he who began a good work in you will bring it to completion at the day of Jesus Christ. It is right for me to feel this way about you all, because I hold you in my heart, for you are all partakers with me of grace, both in my imprisonment and in the defense and confirmation of the gospel. For God is my witness, how I yearn for you all with the affection of Christ Jesus. And it is my prayer that your love may abound more and more, with knowledge and all discernment, so that you may approve what is excellent, and so be pure and blameless for the day of Christ, filled with the fruit of righteousness that comes through Jesus Christ, to the glory and praise of God.

Reflect:

Paul's consistent and joyful prayers over the Philippians stemmed from his confidence that God would finish what he had started. God was the one who planted the gospel deep within the Philippians. He was the one bringing forth fruit in them now, and he would grow them into perfected, mature believers at the day of Christ.

Is this your confidence when you pray for yourself and other believers?

God will be faithful to grow the seeds he has planted in us. We can pray with this same kind of joyful confidence in God's commitment to our wholeness, our flourishing, and our maturity as his people.

Paul went on to write that he loved this church with the affection of Jesus Christ. Pause and consider: How often can you say that about other people in your life? Rather than feeling condemned over a perceived lack of Christlike love, think of Paul's statement as an invitation. God can form us into people who love other people with the very love of Jesus! What was true for Paul can be true for you and me. We can know the deep, powerful love of Christ for fellow believers.

What did this deep love of Christ compel Paul to do? It compelled him to pray the kind of rich, piercing, poignant prayer that we find in verses 9–11:

> And it is my prayer that your love may abound more and more, with knowledge and all discernment, so that you may approve what is excellent, and so be pure and blameless for the day of Christ, filled with the fruit of righteousness that comes through Jesus Christ, to the glory and praise of God.

As you come before the Lord, ask that God will do this for you and others.

Pray:

O, make your Word a swift Word, passing from the ear to the heart, from the heart to the lip and conversation; that, as the rain returns not empty, so neither may your Word, but accomplish that for which it is given. Amen.

(George Herbert)

Eastertide Day 25

KARI WEST

Read: *Philippians 1:12–18*

I want you to know, brothers, that what has happened to me has really served to advance the gospel, so that it has become known throughout the whole imperial guard and to all the rest that my imprisonment is for Christ. And most of the brothers, having become confident in the Lord by my imprisonment, are much more bold to speak the word without fear.

Some indeed preach Christ from envy and rivalry, but others from good will. The latter do it out of love, knowing that I am put here for the defense of the gospel. The former proclaim Christ out of selfish ambition, not sincerely but thinking to afflict me in my imprisonment. What then? Only that in every way, whether in pretense or in truth, Christ is proclaimed, and in that I rejoice.

Reflect:

Paul was in chains as he penned this letter to the church at Philippi. And yet he called to mind reason after reason to rejoice. In the preceding verses, he was full of joy over the Philippians' partnership in the gospel and over God's commitment to continue his good work in them.

In these verses, we find that Paul rejoiced that Christ was being honored through his imprisonment. Paul saw how his suffering was furthering the kingdom of God. He peered past his present difficulties to find a deeper purpose to what was happening to him.

All the prison guards knew that Paul was in chains because of his commitment to Jesus. More and more believers were compelled to preach the gospel boldly because of Paul's faithful witness. And even though some were proclaiming the gospel from wrong motives, Paul still rejoiced that the message of Christ was reaching farther and farther into the world.

What trials lie before you today? What difficulties are strewn across this season of your life? Will you come before the Lord and ask him to fill your mind and heart with reasons for rejoicing? Will you ask for the faith to peer past what you are experiencing and to hope in the deeper things that God promises to work in your life?

We aren't promised an easy road, but we are promised an ever-present helper. Call out to him and ask for the eyes of faith, for joy, and for a heart that treasures the gospel. Trust that he hears you. Trust that he cares. Trust that he will always do good for you in the end.

As you end your time of prayer, speak the words of this beloved hymn aloud and receive these promises from your heavenly Father:

Pray:

When through fiery trials your pathway shall lie,
My grace, all-sufficient, shall be your supply;
The flame shall not hurt you, I only design
Your dross to consume and the gold to refine.
The soul that on Jesus has leaned for repose
I will not, I will not desert to its foes;
That soul, though all hell should endeavor to shake
I'll never, no never, no never forsake. Amen.

("How Firm a Foundation" by John Rippon)

Eastertide Day 26

KARI WEST

Read: *Philippians 1:18–26*

Yes, and I will rejoice, for I know that through your prayers and the help of the Spirit of Jesus Christ this will turn out for my deliverance, as it is my eager expectation and hope that I will not be at all ashamed, but that with full courage now as always Christ will be honored in my body, whether by life or by death. For to me to live is Christ, and to die is gain. If I am to live in the flesh, that means fruitful labor for me. Yet which I shall choose I cannot tell. I am hard pressed between the two. My desire is to depart and be with Christ, for that is far better. But to remain in the flesh is more necessary on your account. Convinced of this, I know that I will remain and continue with you all, for your progress and joy in the faith, so that in me you may have ample cause to glory in Christ Jesus, because of my coming to you again.

Reflect:

What comes to mind when you think about death?

Can you even consider it, or does your mind quickly grasp hold of any fleeting distraction? Paul was imprisoned as he wrote these words to the Philippians. It seemed as though he had taken time to contemplate the possibility of his imminent death. What was his conclusion?

It's a far better thing to die and be with Jesus in fullness. How could Paul proclaim something so remarkable, so counterintuitive? Death is the enemy, 1 Corinthians 15:26 reminds us. Death is the wage paid for sin. It is a fearful, terrible thing. Anyone who has lost a loved one can feel the wrongness of death. No matter how many times it brushes our lives, it always feels like a monstrous aberration.

The only thing that makes death bearable is our risen Savior standing on the other side of it, declaring a victory over death that is so complete that the only way to describe it is as death being "swallowed up in victory"

(1 Corinthians 15:54). A day is coming when no vestige of death will remain. Even now Jesus holds the keys to the grave. We are not the evil one's captives, even as we die.

And because Jesus stands there, waiting to embrace us and draw us into the utter magnificence of his full presence, it is a far, far better thing to die. Are you fearful of death? We worship the one who trampled that old enemy. It need not hold sway over you, beloved of Jesus.

As you pray, ask our resurrected Lord for such a trust in his goodness, grace, and glory that you can proclaim with Paul: To live is Christ, and to die is gain.

Pray:

O Lord, who is as the shadow of a great rock in a weary land, who beholds your weak creatures, weary of labor, weary of pleasure, weary of hope deferred, weary of self, in your abundant compassion and unutterable tenderness, bring us, we ask you, unto your rest. Amen.

(Christina Rossetti)

Eastertide Day 27

KARI WEST

Read: *Philippians 1:27–30*

> Only let your manner of life be worthy of the gospel of Christ, so that whether I come and see you or am absent, I may hear of you that you are standing firm in one spirit, with one mind striving side by side for the faith of the gospel, and not frightened in anything by your opponents. This is a clear sign to them of their destruction, but of your salvation, and that from God. For it has been granted to you that for the sake of Christ you should not only believe in him but also suffer for his sake, engaged in the same conflict that you saw I had and now hear that I still have.

Reflect:

"Whatever happens," Paul urged the Philippians, "conduct yourselves in a manner worthy of the gospel of Christ" (Philippians 1:27 NIV). "Whatever happens" is quite the all-encompassing phrase. Paul believed that through all our circumstances, trials, emotional upheavals, and successes or failures, we could conduct ourselves in a manner worthy of the gospel.

How does that sit with you? Does that idea draw up disbelief, cynicism, or guilt in you? Does it feel like an impossible standard to reach? Take those feelings before the Lord.

The truth is, we can embrace these words of Paul as a promise. It is God who saves us, and it is God's power that works within us. If we offer up our lives to him—hourly and daily—asking him to transform us, he will take our offering and do as we request. No trial, no emotional turmoil, and no days of drudgery have the ultimate ability to keep us from living lives worthy of the gospel.

And what is the result of this kind of life? Paul revealed this earlier in his prayer over the Philippians: We are "filled with the fruit of righteousness that comes through Jesus Christ, to the glory and praise of God" (Philippians 1:11).

Fruit is a sign of rich soil, of deep roots, of true life, of a wise and worthy gardener. The fruit of righteousness in our lives comes through the power of the Lord Jesus as we continually bow our knee to him and his kingdom rule, to the glory and the praise of God.

As you pray, ask for a renewed love of God's Word and trust in his power. Confess the ways you live that do not adorn the gospel. Submit again to Christ's lordship and praise him for his faithfulness to you.

Pray:
Go, then, earthly fame and treasure!
Come disaster, scorn and pain!
In Thy service, pain is pleasure,
With Thy favor, loss is gain.
I have called Thee Abba, Father;
I have stayed my heart on Thee.
Storms may howl, and clouds may gather.
All must work for good to me. Amen.

("Jesus, I My Cross Have Taken" by Henry Francis Lyte)

Eastertide Day 28
SALLY BREEDLOVE

Read: *Philippians 2:5–8*

Have this mind among yourselves, which is yours in Christ Jesus, who, though he was in the form of God, did not count equality with God a thing to be grasped, but emptied himself, by taking the form of a servant, being born in the likeness of men. And being found in human form, he humbled himself by becoming obedient to the point of death, even death on a cross.

Reflect:

In the ancient world, foot washing was a necessity. Roads were dusty and muddy, and animals walked the same paths and roads that people did. Not everyone wore shoes, and most shoes were only sandals. It was a matter of hygiene and comfort to provide a way for people to wash their feet when they entered a home. If you had any means, you provided a servant to do the job for your guests or family.

But at the Last Supper, the Eternal Son of God stripped down like a servant to wash his disciples' feet even as they were jostling among themselves over who deserved first place with Jesus.

Peter protested that Jesus would not wash his feet. Jesus insisted. Then, as he finished and sat down among his stunned and chastised disciples, he explained what he had done. "You call me Teacher and Lord, and you are right, for so I am. If I then, your Lord and Teacher, have washed your feet, you also ought to wash one another's feet. For I have given you an example, that you also should do just as I have done to you" (John 13:13–15).

Jesus invites us to follow him and take a servant's place. Look around you. You will see the presence of Christ being lived out in choices other people are making.

Will you pray in thanksgiving for those who serve as Christ serves? When you chafe against life as it is? Will you pray and ask God for specific ways you can serve our world?

Will you hold Christ's words and pray that he makes your heart like his? "For even the Son of Man came not to be served but to serve, and to give his life as a ransom for many" (Mark 10:45).

Pray:

O Lord our God, whose blessed Son gave his back to be whipped and did not hide his face from shame and spitting: Give us grace to accept joyfully the sufferings of the present time, confident of the glory that shall be revealed; through Jesus Christ our Lord, who lives and reigns with you and the Holy Spirit, one God, for ever and ever. Amen.

(Anglican Church in North America Book of Common Prayer)

Fifth Sunday of Easter
BRANDON WALSH

Read: *Psalm 63*

> O God, you are my God; earnestly I seek you;
>> my soul thirsts for you;
> my flesh faints for you,
>> as in a dry and weary land where there is no water.
> So I have looked upon you in the sanctuary,
>> beholding your power and glory.
> Because your steadfast love is better than life,
>> my lips will praise you.
> So I will bless you as long as I live;
>> in your name I will lift up my hands.
> My soul will be satisfied as with fat and rich food,
>> and my mouth will praise you with joyful lips,
> when I remember you upon my bed,
>> and meditate on you in the watches of the night;
> for you have been my help,
>> and in the shadow of your wings I will sing for joy.
> My soul clings to you;
>> your right hand upholds me.
> But those who seek to destroy my life
>> shall go down into the depths of the earth;
> they shall be given over to the power of the sword;
>> they shall be a portion for jackals.
> But the king shall rejoice in God;
>> all who swear by him shall exult,
>> for the mouths of liars will be stopped.

Reflect:

Sometimes we read a text like this and think, *I wish I felt that way about God.*

But what if there is another way to read these words? What if these words give us a clue about what we are really hungry for? What if these words in Psalm 63 express the state of our souls more clearly than we can feel or articulate? What if it's just a fact that our soul thirsts for God and that our flesh faints for him (vv. 1, 3)?

We might be living our whole lives hungry for something that we can't quite name or accomplish. We might be going through life as if we are making a hungry trip to the grocery store—forever seeing things with hungry and thirsty eyes. Our hunger for satisfaction shapes how we see the people and things around us.

We enter the world doing hungry math. Our hearts are restless, thirsty, and faint until we find our rest and satisfaction in the Lord.

As you pray, ponder your own deep hunger. Confess to God your longing for him.

Pray:

O God, of your goodness, give me yourself, for you are enough for me. I can ask for nothing less that is completely to your honor, and if I do ask anything less, I shall always be in want. Only in you I have all. Amen.

(Julian of Norwich)

Eastertide Day 30
KARI WEST

Read: *Philippians 2:12–18*

> Therefore, my beloved, as you have always obeyed, so now, not only as in my presence but much more in my absence, work out your own salvation with fear and trembling, for it is God who works in you, both to will and to work for his good pleasure.
>
> Do all things without grumbling or disputing, that you may be blameless and innocent, children of God without blemish in the midst of a crooked and twisted generation, among whom you shine as lights in the world, holding fast to the word of life, so that in the day of Christ I may be proud that I did not run in vain or labor in vain. Even if I am to be poured out as a drink offering upon the sacrificial offering of your faith, I am glad and rejoice with you all. Likewise you also should be glad and rejoice with me.

Reflect:

There is a connection between joyful, contented living and firmly holding to the Word of life, namely, Christ. That connection can't be severed by personal hardships or the crookedness of the world around us. That connection keeps us from devolving into the natural responses of complaining and grumbling when life is difficult.

If we are wholly alone in suffering and hardship, if all we can see is the darkness in our world, then complaining and grumbling would be an understandable response to the times in which we live. But Paul called us to put away complaining and arguing when we face hardship and a bleak world. How can we accomplish this?

Paul said he was able to rejoice because holding on to Christ brings joy. He rejoiced because a life of holding on to Christ is never in vain. He was honest about this life being one of service; it felt like being poured out as a drink offering. It was full of intense sacrificial work. But this kind of life is possible because Paul hoped in the day of Christ and in the coming of the King.

It can be the same for us today. Are you facing a season of deep trial, of sleeplessness, of anxiety, of pain? Hold on to Jesus, and more importantly, know that he holds you. He will work in you his good will. Christ is King, and he will come again.

As you pray, confess your grumbling. Ask for a fresh awareness of the abiding presence of Christ and ask for the strength to rest in his sovereign love for you.

Pray:

Do grant that your Spirit may take away the old man with his affections and lusts, and renew us in the spirit of our minds, and enable us to put on the new man which is created in righteousness and true holiness. Grant that we may be enabled more and more to display those fruits and effects of your Holy Spirit which we find in the character of your first disciples. Give us the administration of the Spirit according to our respective necessities. May we abound in every Christian grace, and thus know that we are branches in the living Vine. May we glorify our heavenly Father, and receive from you whatever is needful for our bodies and our souls. Amen.

(William Wilberforce)

Eastertide Day 31
SALLY BREEDLOVE

Read: *Philippians 3:7–21*

> But whatever gain I had, I counted as loss for the sake of Christ. Indeed, I count everything as loss because of the surpassing worth of knowing Christ Jesus my Lord. For his sake I have suffered the loss of all things and count them as rubbish, in order that I may gain Christ and be found in him, not having a righteousness of my own that comes from the law, but that which comes through faith in Christ, the righteousness from God that depends on faith—that I may know him and the power of his resurrection, and may share his sufferings, becoming like him in his death, that by any means possible I may attain the resurrection from the dead.
>
> Not that I have already obtained this or am already perfect, but I press on to make it my own, because Christ Jesus has made me his own. Brothers, I do not consider that I have made it my own. But one thing I do: forgetting what lies behind and straining forward to what lies ahead, I press on toward the goal for the prize of the upward call of God in Christ Jesus. Let those of us who are mature think this way, and if in anything you think otherwise, God will reveal that also to you. Only let us hold true to what we have attained.
>
> Brothers, join in imitating me, and keep your eyes on those who walk according to the example you have in us. For many, of whom I have often told you and now tell you even with tears, walk as enemies of the cross of Christ. Their end is destruction, their god is their belly, and they glory in their shame, with minds set on earthly things. But our citizenship is in heaven, and from it we await a Savior, the Lord Jesus Christ, who will transform our lowly body to be like his glorious body, by the power that enables him even to subject all things to himself.

Reflect:

What do we have to look forward to in this life? Perhaps you are in a season where the horizon of your future seems to be shrinking. But Paul proclaimed plenty of reasons to stay grounded in hope and confidence no matter what does or doesn't happen in life.

Paul offered us a different way to live when life is hard: Find your joy in the Lord. As Christ faced his own death, he promised to give us joy. Do you believe that? Will you accept the kind of joy he offers? Will you believe Jesus is the only source of unfading happiness?

Stop trusting the things that make you feel that you are secure and important in this world. Paul swept the things we often long for into a trash pile: a flawless life, an important job, the right connections and education. He said to let them go or let them be taken from you. They don't add up to half a thimbleful of joy compared to knowing Jesus.

Paul called us to know Jesus more fully. We need humility since none of us will arrive at a full knowledge of Christ on this side of heaven. But we can be hopeful because Jesus has laid hold of us, and he'll never let us go.

And finally, Paul encouraged us to follow and imitate godly leaders.

Whom do you want to be like? We are called to live in a new way, but the heart of joy is about something beyond this present brief life. Our real joy is that we are citizens (already!) of heaven and we are waiting for our Savior King to arrive.

As you pray, listen to this counsel from the apostle Paul. What do you need to pick up or put down to know joy, even in a world like ours? Take a minute to thank God that one day when Jesus comes, we will know joy in full.

Pray:

Give me, O Lord, a steadfast heart, which no unworthy thought can drag down; an unconquered heart, which no tribulation can wear out; an upright heart, which no unworthy purpose can tempt aside. Bestow upon me understanding to know you, diligence to seek you, wisdom to find you, and faithfulness that finally may embrace you. Amen.

(Thomas Aquinas)

Eastertide Day 32

SALLY BREEDLOVE

Read: *Philippians 4:4–13*

Rejoice in the Lord always; again I will say, rejoice. Let your reasonableness be known to everyone. The Lord is at hand; do not be anxious about anything, but in everything by prayer and supplication with thanksgiving let your requests be made known to God. And the peace of God, which surpasses all understanding, will guard your hearts and your minds in Christ Jesus.

Finally, brothers, whatever is true, whatever is honorable, whatever is just, whatever is pure, whatever is lovely, whatever is commendable, if there is any excellence, if there is anything worthy of praise, think about these things. What you have learned and received and heard and seen in me—practice these things, and the God of peace will be with you.

I rejoiced in the Lord greatly that now at length you have revived your concern for me. You were indeed concerned for me, but you had no opportunity. Not that I am speaking of being in need, for I have learned in whatever situation I am to be content. I know how to be brought low, and I know how to abound. In any and every circumstance, I have learned the secret of facing plenty and hunger, abundance and need. I can do all things through him who strengthens me.

Reflect:

The way Paul described prayer in this passage might be summed up like this: *Ask God for whatever you want and thank him for whatever he gives.* Paul didn't say, "Tell God the things a good Christian would tell him," or "Ask in the right way and you will get it." No, it is far simpler. Be like a child—turn your desires (as confused or misshapen or small as they may be) into prayers to our holy God. Then receive with gratitude what he gives you.

Ponder the call to think about good things and imitate the actions and words of godly people. Our minds so quickly slip out of alignment, and we fall back into our favorite rut of fear, envy, or resentment. A desire to corral our thoughts is like the desire to herd cats: largely impossible. It is far better, Paul said, to choose something else to think about, something good and true. Notice what you are thinking about, and then shift your focus to things that are lovely and honorable. Then choose to act like people you admire, whether you feel like it or not.

Consider your own circumstances. Your life may be too large or too small, too challenging or too boring, too full or too empty. But ask yourself: Is the life you've been given enough? Even if it is small, or damaged, or limited, God is so very present with you. Contentment is saying to God, "Thank you. I have enough. You are with me, which is more than plenty." Even when everything in you rages that you deserve more, saying thank you for everything you possibly can takes you back to contentment and back to God.

Our life with God is shaped by prayer, contemplation, acceptance, and thanksgiving. Not everything in our story is good, but it is all held in the hands of the good and beautiful God.

In the middle of whatever hardships we face, Christ invites us to open up our hearts to joy. As you pray, do just that—pour out your heart to God. Be as honest and grateful as you can possibly be. He will be enough.

Pray:
O Lord God, we can no other answer make than thanks and thanks and ever thanks, because of Christ Jesus. Amen.

Eastertide Day 33
SALLY BREEDLOVE

Read: *Colossians 1:3–8, 15–20*

We always thank God, the Father of our Lord Jesus Christ, when we pray for you, since we heard of your faith in Christ Jesus and of the love that you have for all the saints, because of the hope laid up for you in heaven. Of this you have heard before in the word of the truth, the gospel, which has come to you, as indeed in the whole world it is bearing fruit and increasing—as it also does among you, since the day you heard it and understood the grace of God in truth, just as you learned it from Epaphras our beloved fellow servant. He is a faithful minister of Christ on your behalf and has made known to us your love in the Spirit....

He is the image of the invisible God, the firstborn of all creation. For by him all things were created, in heaven and on earth, visible and invisible, whether thrones or dominions or rulers or authorities—all things were created through him and for him. And he is before all things, and in him all things hold together. And he is the head of the body, the church. He is the beginning, the firstborn from the dead, that in everything he might be preeminent. For in him all the fullness of God was pleased to dwell, and through him to reconcile to himself all things, whether on earth or in heaven, making peace by the blood of his cross.

Reflect:

What about this world would you love to see changed? What have you had enough of? Be honest as you listen to your own heart. We live in a world that keeps receiving more of the same bad news at the turn of every season.

Perhaps you need to take ten steps away from the latest crisis or dire prediction and remind yourself of the big picture. Colossians says Jesus was supreme in the beginning and will be supreme in the end. We, on the other hand, may be in the middle of deep difficulty and struggle. Our strength will come from seeing the whole story and living into it.

What is the real story? The triune God has always been and will always be. As Jesus himself declared in Revelation 1:8, he is "the Alpha and the Omega." In his great goodness, he created a beautiful cosmos where his kingship would bless everything he made. But rather than responding with gratitude, we chose mutiny and rebellion. Our rejection of his kingship still spreads out like shock waves from an earthquake. The result? We live in a broken and dislocated universe where few know their meaning or place.

Paul also experienced this tension, but he did not despair. In Jesus, God rescues people who will join him in this work of reestablishing the rightful rule of King Jesus.

It sounds cosmic (and it is), but it is also personal and ordinary. It is listening to someone you disagree with. It is acting with compassion rather than ignoring the need of another. It is responding with kindness when insulted. It is choosing humility rather than standing on your rights. It is delighting that the King is near and will one day come in fullness.

Today—this, another day in the middle—matters. Live this day for that day when the King will come in fullness. As you pray, ask God for one specific way you can live out the prayer "Your kingdom come, your will be done."

Pray:

O God, grant that we may desire you, and desiring you seek you, and seeking you find you, and finding you be satisfied in you for ever. Amen.

(Francis of Xavier)

Eastertide Day 34

SALLY BREEDLOVE

Read: *Colossians 1:9–12*

> And so, from the day we heard, we have not ceased to pray for you, asking that you may be filled with the knowledge of his will in all spiritual wisdom and understanding, so as to walk in a manner worthy of the Lord, fully pleasing to him: bearing fruit in every good work and increasing in the knowledge of God; being strengthened with all power, according to his glorious might, for all endurance and patience with joy; giving thanks to the Father, who has qualified you to share in the inheritance of the saints in light.

Reflect:

Every day, we are faced with the same fundamental decision: whether or not to walk with our Savior in simple obedience. Do we walk "in a manner worthy of the Lord"? Are we bearing fruit in every good work? Are we increasing in the knowledge of God? Are we being strengthened with all power and filled with patience and joy?

God wants far more for us than to hunker down and make it through. This passage invites us to give up the "grim strength of gritting [our] teeth" and to accept instead the "glory-strength God gives"—a strength that "endures the unendurable and spills over into joy" (MSG). Each one of us can enter our Savior's joy. His joy is a balm to our exhausting striving; it dismantles the fantasy of wishful thinking that we can somehow be enough on our own. When we labor with this strength, we will know a profound peace. The Spirit wants to bind the church together in this strength.

Will you join the Spirit in praying for yourself in this way? How do you long to be strengthened? How has God shown you goodness even in difficulty? Thank him for the goodness in your life, just as it is right now. Ask him to give you joy and strength.

Finally, turn your attention to those you love. What strength do you long for them to have? Pray what you notice back to your Father.

176

Pray:

Come, Holy Spirit, and bring from heaven a ray of your light! Come, you father of the poor, you giver of gifts, you light of the world, the blessed comforter, the dear guest of the soul, and its sweetest refreshment; you, our repose in labor, our coolness in heat, our comfort in affliction! O, most blessed Spirit; fill full the hearts of your faithful people! Without your influence there is nothing in man which is not weakness and guilt. O, cleanse that which is sordid; water that which is dried up; heal that which is wounded; bend that which is stubborn; cherish in your bosom that which is cold; guide that which is wandering; and grant unto your servants, putting their trust in you, the merit of your righteousness; grant them final salvation; grant them everlasting joy! O Lord, hear our prayer, and let our cry come to you. Amen.

(Bernard of Clairvaux)

Eastertide Day 35
SALLY BREEDLOVE

Read: *Colossians 1:21–2:5*

And you, who once were alienated and hostile in mind, doing evil deeds, he has now reconciled in his body of flesh by his death, in order to present you holy and blameless and above reproach before him, if indeed you continue in the faith, stable and steadfast, not shifting from the hope of the gospel that you heard, which has been proclaimed in all creation under heaven, and of which I, Paul, became a minister.

Now I rejoice in my sufferings for your sake, and in my flesh I am filling up what is lacking in Christ's afflictions for the sake of his body, that is, the church, of which I became a minister according to the stewardship from God that was given to me for you, to make the word of God fully known, the mystery hidden for ages and generations but now revealed to his saints. To them God chose to make known how great among the Gentiles are the riches of the glory of this mystery, which is Christ in you, the hope of glory. Him we proclaim, warning everyone and teaching everyone with all wisdom, that we may present everyone mature in Christ. For this I toil, struggling with all his energy that he powerfully works within me.

For I want you to know how great a struggle I have for you and for those at Laodicea and for all who have not seen me face to face, that their hearts may be encouraged, being knit together in love, to reach all the riches of full assurance of understanding and the knowledge of God's mystery, which is Christ, in whom are hidden all the treasures of wisdom and knowledge. I say this in order that no one may delude you with plausible arguments. For though I am absent in body, yet I am with you in spirit, rejoicing to see your good order and the firmness of your faith in Christ.

Reflect:

Paul didn't pull any punches, did he?

Paul was a citizen in the most sophisticated empire of his time. He was a highly educated Jew in a culture that valued reading, thought, and dialogue. By the end of his life, he was widely traveled and had debated and presented the work of Jesus from the Areopagus in Athens to the courts of kings; he had shared the gospel with everyone from slave girls and wealthy women to the Praetorian Guard who worked for Caesar in Rome. But he never changed his tune. It was always, always Jesus.

Paul's passion was to develop Christ-followers whose lives were deeply centered and established on Jesus. The truth, Paul said, is in Jesus alone. The truth *is* Jesus. He declared that he gladly participated in the suffering of Jesus—in Jesus's rejection, in his sorrow over the broken lostness of the world, in his laying down of his own life for the world.

We live in a world that is simultaneously intrigued by spiritual things and yet squeamish if we say, "Jesus Christ, God come in the flesh, is the center of all." Paul, however, was blunt: "The mystery in a nutshell is just this: Christ is in you, so therefore you can look forward to sharing in God's glory. It's that simple. That is the substance of our Message" (Colossians 1:27 MSG).

Maturity is the profound simplicity found in clinging to Jesus. We can wake up trusting that Jesus is the center of the universe and that he holds all things together. We can be confident of Jesus and live our day seeking to be poured out for the sake of others. As you come to him in prayer, rest in these certainties.

Pray:

O Lord Jesus, help me to remember that the sufferings of this present world are not worthy to be compared to the glory that awaits us when your kingdom comes in fullness. Help us to live today for that day; for Jesus Christ's sake. Amen.

Sixth Sunday of Easter
BRANDON WALSH

Read: *Psalm 67*

> May God be gracious to us and bless us
> > and make his face to shine upon us,   *Selah*
> that your way may be known on earth,
> > your saving power among all nations.
> Let the peoples praise you, O God;
> > let all the peoples praise you!
> Let the nations be glad and sing for joy,
> > for you judge the peoples with equity
> > and guide the nations upon earth.   *Selah*
> Let the peoples praise you, O God;
> > let all the peoples praise you!
> The earth has yielded its increase;
> > God, our God, shall bless us.
> God shall bless us;
> > let all the ends of the earth fear him!

Reflect:

A tension exists throughout the Old Testament between the elect people of God and God's divine purpose for all the nations. God chose Abraham as the one through whom all nations will be blessed. But Abraham had to bear that promise and be the avenue through which the particular blessings of God flowed.

In Psalm 67, the psalmist desired election and the blessings and graciousness of the Lord, not simply for Israel but for the ultimate purposes of God: He longed for Yahweh to be known throughout the whole world, that the nations might sing and be glad. The blessings of God for the people of Israel had a purpose beyond the well-being of his people. It was a blessing for the sake of the world.

In the same way, the Lord shares his Spirit abundantly with us. We pray that the Lord might turn his face toward us and bless us. However, all the blessings we receive are not for us alone but for the sake of the world. The vocation—the calling—of Israel was to be a light to the nations, a place where peoples looked and saw something different. Jesus continued that image in the Sermon on the Mount, calling us to be a city on a hill and salt and light in the world.

Beyond anything else, Christ's greatest gift to the church is himself—his own life—and he is the light of humankind. In Christ, the Lord turns his face toward us as he invites us to go forth into all the world both to proclaim and to *be* that good news. The gift of Christ and the Holy Spirit is not simply a balm to make us feel better, but oil in our lamps to light the way for others.

As you pray, pray that your life might be a conduit of blessing to others.

Pray:

O God, our heavenly Father, you manifested your love by sending your only-begotten Son into the world, that all might live through him: Pour out your Spirit on your Church, that we may fulfill his command to preach the Gospel to all people. Send forth laborers into your harvest; defend them in all dangers and temptations; and hasten the time when the fullness of the Gentiles shall be gathered in, and faithful Israel shall be saved; through your Son Jesus Christ our Lord. Amen.

(Anglican Church in North America Book of Common Prayer)

Eastertide Day 37
SALLY BREEDLOVE

Read: *Colossians 2:6–19*

Therefore, as you received Christ Jesus the Lord, so walk in him, rooted and built up in him and established in the faith, just as you were taught, abounding in thanksgiving.

See to it that no one takes you captive by philosophy and empty deceit, according to human tradition, according to the elemental spirits of the world, and not according to Christ. For in him the whole fullness of deity dwells bodily, and you have been filled in him, who is the head of all rule and authority. In him also you were circumcised with a circumcision made without hands, by putting off the body of the flesh, by the circumcision of Christ, having been buried with him in baptism, in which you were also raised with him through faith in the powerful working of God, who raised him from the dead. And you, who were dead in your trespasses and the uncircumcision of your flesh, God made alive together with him, having forgiven us all our trespasses, by canceling the record of debt that stood against us with its legal demands. This he set aside, nailing it to the cross. He disarmed the rulers and authorities and put them to open shame, by triumphing over them in him.

Therefore let no one pass judgment on you in questions of food and drink, or with regard to a festival or a new moon or a Sabbath. These are a shadow of the things to come, but the substance belongs to Christ. Let no one disqualify you, insisting on asceticism and worship of angels, going on in detail about visions, puffed up without reason by his sensuous mind, and not holding fast to the Head, from whom the whole body, nourished and knit together through its joints and ligaments, grows with a growth that is from God.

Reflect:

Listen to how *The Message* puts Paul's words in Colossians 2:10: "You don't need a telescope, a microscope, or a horoscope to realize the fullness of Christ, and the emptiness of the universe without him. When you come to him, that fullness comes together for you, too."

We are people of longings, which begin at birth. We are thrust into this world, and we long for air, for milk, for warmth, for closeness, and for touch. Without longings, are we really human?

Paul told the Colossians that because of Jesus, they belonged in God's family. But it's not just belonging we desire—we want to know we are wanted and that we are good enough to be accepted as daughters and sons. Paul assured us that we measure up because of Jesus's death on the cross and our baptism into his life.

We are insiders because of Christ, but it doesn't stop there. We don't need to concoct a self-improvement course in order to maintain our place in God's family. Special diets, rituals, and secret knowledge all add up to nothing in God's eyes. Grace and mercy are so very large that Christ is always enough.

It's all too easy to feel isolated and to slide into loneliness and self-doubt about our worthiness. As you pray, turn away from those thoughts. Listen to the real truth about yourself and about the overflowing love of Jesus Christ. Thank your Father God that you belong to Jesus, to his family, and to his grand purposes in this world. No matter what else you have or don't have, know that you have Christ and that he is enough.

Pray:

I cannot, O God, stand in the day of battle and danger, unless you cover me with your shield, and hide me under your wings. You did make me after your image; be pleased to preserve me so pure and spotless, that my body may be a holy temple, and my soul a sanctuary to entertain your most divine Spirit, the Spirit of love and holiness. Amen.

(Jeremy Taylor)

Eastertide Day 38
SALLY BREEDLOVE

Read: *Colossians 2:20–3:11*

If with Christ you died to the elemental spirits of the world, why, as if you were still alive in the world, do you submit to regulations—"Do not handle, Do not taste, Do not touch" (referring to things that all perish as they are used)—according to human precepts and teachings? These have indeed an appearance of wisdom in promoting self-made religion and asceticism and severity to the body, but they are of no value in stopping the indulgence of the flesh.

If then you have been raised with Christ, seek the things that are above, where Christ is, seated at the right hand of God. Set your minds on things that are above, not on things that are on earth. For you have died, and your life is hidden with Christ in God. When Christ who is your life appears, then you also will appear with him in glory.

Put to death therefore what is earthly in you: sexual immorality, impurity, passion, evil desire, and covetousness, which is idolatry. On account of these the wrath of God is coming. In these you too once walked, when you were living in them. But now you must put them all away: anger, wrath, malice, slander, and obscene talk from your mouth. Do not lie to one another, seeing that you have put off the old self with its practices and have put on the new self, which is being renewed in knowledge after the image of its creator. Here there is not Greek and Jew, circumcised and uncircumcised, barbarian, Scythian, slave, free; but Christ is all, and in all.

Reflect:

In the preceding chapters of Colossians, Paul urged us to realize that a life full of rituals and insider religious talk is not at all what life in Jesus is like. Here he continued that theme as he focused on our character and everyday choices.

The bottom line? Once we come to Jesus, our hearts and minds should no longer be focused on things or feelings instead of on God. That kind of short-sighted focus stirs up everything from sexual promiscuity to a bad temper in us.

The solution, Paul made clear, is not doubling down on a self-congratulating self-discipline about outward things that perish and don't matter in the long run. Fastidious choices about what we do or don't do, or what we eat or don't eat, may make us look pious, humble, or ascetic, but they don't deal with our self-serving and self-deceived hearts. As Jesus told us in Luke 6:45, "Out of the abundance of the heart his mouth speaks."

As you begin your time of prayer, pause and consider: What fills your heart and your mind as you go about your day? Where do you wish you could make different choices from the ones you consistently make? What thoughts or emotions plague you that you can't shake off? How do you long to change?

Paul's counsel makes such good sense. Christ has given you his resurrection life, so look up, be alert, and see life from Christ's perspective.

Praise God as you pray. It is his life in you that will remake you. Welcome him in the work he is doing.

Pray:

What I do, make me do, simply as your child; let me be, throughout the day, as a child in his loving father's presence, ever looking up to you. May I love you for all your love. May I thank you, if not in words, yet in my heart, for each gift of your love, for each comfort which you allow me day by day. Amen.

(E. B. Pusey)

Eastertide Day 39
SALLY BREEDLOVE

Read: *Colossians 3:12-25*

Put on then, as God's chosen ones, holy and beloved, compassionate hearts, kindness, humility, meekness, and patience, bearing with one another and, if one has a complaint against another, forgiving each other; as the Lord has forgiven you, so you also must forgive. And above all these put on love, which binds everything together in perfect harmony. And let the peace of Christ rule in your hearts, to which indeed you were called in one body. And be thankful. Let the word of Christ dwell in you richly, teaching and admonishing one another in all wisdom, singing psalms and hymns and spiritual songs, with thankfulness in your hearts to God. And whatever you do, in word or deed, do everything in the name of the Lord Jesus, giving thanks to God the Father through him.

Wives, submit to your husbands, as is fitting in the Lord. Husbands, love your wives, and do not be harsh with them. Children, obey your parents in everything, for this pleases the Lord. Fathers, do not provoke your children, lest they become discouraged. Bondservants, obey in everything those who are your earthly masters, not by way of eye-service, as people-pleasers, but with sincerity of heart, fearing the Lord. Whatever you do, work heartily, as for the Lord and not for men, knowing that from the Lord you will receive the inheritance as your reward. You are serving the Lord Christ. For the wrongdoer will be paid back for the wrong he has done, and there is no partiality.

Reflect:

The end goal of the Christian life is to be remade so we are like our Master, our Friend, our Savior, our big brother Jesus Christ. What does it mean to be like Jesus? Paul said in this passage that it is to live a life of love.

Isn't it easy to want something else even as we follow Jesus? Even if we never speak it out loud, we find it easy to believe that we must have something in addition to Jesus. If only we had success, a church we really liked, a spouse or a better spouse, children, grown children out of the house, a job that really mattered, the right political party in power, or freedom from fear of disease, then we could better follow the command to walk in love.

But Paul made it clear that love is fundamental. Love is the one thing we need: "It's your basic, all-purpose garment. Never be without it" (Colossians 3:14 MSG).

The truth about love is that it begins with a litany of small but radical choices: living deeply in the Scriptures day by day so they guide your understanding of life; singing joyfully and choosing to be thankful, even when your heart is heavy; embracing the peace of Christ even when others offend you; and determining to serve others in the everyday relationships of your life.

Paul put it in stark terms in 1 Corinthians 13: Without love we are nothing. As you pray, ask God to teach you to love as he loves.

Pray:
Lord, make me an instrument of your peace.
Where there is hatred, let me bring love.
Where there is offense, let me bring pardon.
Where there is discord, let me bring union.
Where there is error, let me bring truth.
Where there is doubt, let me bring faith.
Where there is despair, let me bring hope.
Where there is darkness, let me bring your light.
Where there is sadness, let me bring joy.
O Master, let me not seek as much to be consoled as to console,
to be understood as to understand, to be loved as to love,
for it is in giving that one receives, it is in self-forgetting that one finds,
it is in pardoning that one is pardoned,
it is in dying that one is raised to eternal life. Amen.
(Francis of Assisi)

Ascension Day: Eastertide Day 40
BRANDON WALSH

Read: *Acts 1:1–11*

> In the first book, O Theophilus, I have dealt with all that Jesus began to do and teach, until the day when he was taken up, after he had given commands through the Holy Spirit to the apostles whom he had chosen. He presented himself alive to them after his suffering by many proofs, appearing to them during forty days and speaking about the kingdom of God.
>
> And while staying with them he ordered them not to depart from Jerusalem, but to wait for the promise of the Father, which, he said, "you heard from me; for John baptized with water, but you will be baptized with the Holy Spirit not many days from now."
>
> So when they had come together, they asked him, "Lord, will you at this time restore the kingdom to Israel?" He said to them, "It is not for you to know times or seasons that the Father has fixed by his own authority. But you will receive power when the Holy Spirit has come upon you, and you will be my witnesses in Jerusalem and in all Judea and Samaria, and to the end of the earth." And when he had said these things, as they were looking on, he was lifted up, and a cloud took him out of their sight. And while they were gazing into heaven as he went, behold, two men stood by them in white robes, and said, "Men of Galilee, why do you stand looking into heaven? This Jesus, who was taken up from you into heaven, will come in the same way as you saw him go into heaven."

Reflect:

For forty days the resurrected Jesus appeared to the disciples and taught them about the kingdom of God. They had the chance to see Jesus in his glory and, through him to see the world in a whole new light. This period after the resurrection was a crash course in resurrection life.

Luke, the writer of Acts and the Gospel of Luke, addressed the patron of this work, Theophilus (which literally means "lover of God"). As Acts began, Luke told Theophilus that in his Gospel he had recorded what Jesus began to do and teach before his ascension. But Luke knew for certain that the work of Christ was not finished. Christ would send his Spirit to continue his work. The Spirit would empower the disciples to witness to him in Jerusalem, Judea, Samaria, and to the ends of the earth. The book of Acts followed that road map as the resurrection of Jesus sent shock waves across the known world.

It would have been a gift to join the disciples in the forty-day crash course that Jesus offered. But in truth, the class is not over. Jesus didn't stop empowering his disciples and teaching them; he continues to empower and teach his disciples through the Holy Spirit and through one another.

When we open Scripture together, when we share the Lord's Supper, when we rejoice and weep with each other, we are sharing in Christ's presence among us. The Lord is teaching us what it means to live in light of the resurrection, in light of the kingdom he has already inaugurated and will one day fulfill.

As you pray, thank the Lord for the gift of the Spirit, for the gift of the Scriptures, for the gift of other Christians. Pray for freedom to gather as the body of Christ.

Pray:

Soul of Christ, sanctify me. Body of Christ, save me. Blood of Christ, inebriate me. Water from the side of Christ, wash me. Passion of Christ, strengthen me. O good Jesus, hear me. Within thy wounds hide me. Suffer me not to be separated from thee. From the wicked foe defend me. In the hour of my death call me, and bid me come to thee, that with thy saints I may praise thee for ever and ever. Amen.

(Anima Christi)

Eastertide Day 41

STEVEN E. BREEDLOVE

Read: *Acts 1:4–8*

And while staying with them he ordered them not to depart from Jerusalem, but to wait for the promise of the Father, which, he said, "you heard from me; for John baptized with water, but you will be baptized with the Holy Spirit not many days from now."

So when they had come together, they asked him, "Lord, will you at this time restore the kingdom to Israel?" He said to them, "It is not for you to know times or seasons that the Father has fixed by his own authority. But you will receive power when the Holy Spirit has come upon you, and you will be my witnesses in Jerusalem and in all Judea and Samaria, and to the end of the earth."

Reflect:

During Holy Week we seek to walk in the footsteps of Jesus, but as we move from Ascension to Pentecost, we walk in the footsteps of the disciples. Indeed, much of life can feel like learning to walk between Ascension and Pentecost.

At the Ascension, Jesus told the disciples to go to Jerusalem and wait for the power of the Holy Spirit, who would be given by the Father, so that they could accomplish the task to which Christ had called them. The image of the disciples receiving a call and yet having to wait in patience for God's powerful presence fits with much of our experience. The disciples didn't know how long the wait would be and they didn't know what it would be like to receive the presence of the Holy Spirit. They simply had to wait in patience and faith.

We, too, often know that there is something for us to do. Perhaps it's a particular task, job, or goal that we know is ours. Perhaps it's a new spiritual discipline or a deeper level of pursuing God. We know we are called, yet we can't seem to succeed.

Perhaps it is a level of contentment and peace that we desire but cannot achieve on our own strength. Perhaps it is reconciliation of a particular relationship. We all have moments where there is something before us—something from God—that we cannot yet reach. In these moments, we are called, like the disciples, to wait in faith. We are waiting for God to show up, waiting for the strength of the Holy Spirit to do what we are called to do, waiting for the promise to be given.

We don't get to dictate the length of the wait. We don't know what it will be like for God to arrive. We don't know how the calling will be fulfilled. Like the disciples, we are simply called to remain in our particular Jerusalem until God arrives.

As you wait for Pentecost next Sunday, let the fact that we are between Ascension and Pentecost encourage you to keep waiting for the presence of God, who will lead you into the calling he has for you in his timing.

Pray that you will wait with patience and hope, eager for his help.

Pray:

Oh God, the King of glory, you have exalted your only Son Jesus Christ with great triumph to your kingdom in heaven: Do not leave us comfortless, but send us your Holy Spirit to strengthen us and exalt us to that place where your Savior Christ has gone before; who lives and reigns with you and the Holy Spirit, one God, in glory everlasting. Amen.

(Anglican Church in North America Book of Common Prayer)

Eastertide Day 42
SALLY BREEDLOVE

Read: *Matthew 11:28–30 & Hebrews 4:9–11*

"Come to me, all who labor and are heavy laden, and I will give you rest. Take my yoke upon you, and learn from me, for I am gentle and lowly in heart, and you will find rest for your souls. For my yoke is easy, and my burden is light."

So then, there remains a Sabbath rest for the people of God, for whoever has entered God's rest has also rested from his works as God did from his.

Let us therefore strive to enter that rest, so that no one may fall by the same sort of disobedience.

Reflect:

God has always invited us to find rest in him. From the beginning of Genesis, he held out a gift to us: Sabbath rest for the people of God. For centuries, Saturday (for the Jewish people) and Sunday (the Christian Sabbath) were seen as set-apart days.

Yes, the Sabbath has been abused and turned into a legalistic club. But might the Lord be inviting you now to reexamine Sabbath rest?

The Hebrew word for Sabbath means many things, but three meanings stand out. Sabbath means to take a break, to celebrate, and to let the present be imperfect.

Will you take a break and stop checking things off your to-do list for one day? Stopping is one way to trust God and to grow more discerning. How can you make your next Sabbath a day of stopping?

Will you choose to celebrate? Goodness, beauty, and truth have not left this world. Take time to stop and notice the good gifts you've been given. The insight to see and to say thank you is an offering to God that reshapes your life.

And finally, will you let the present be imperfect? Will you accept life as it is? God guarantees a future of joy, but for now, we walk a pilgrim path in a dimly lit valley. Will you submit to its being enough?

You are invited to rest. From the beginning, God has offered rest. In Jesus, he reaffirms that offer. Come to Jesus, run to Jesus, and rest in Jesus. Are you willing to choose a life of regular Sabbath? Will you say yes to God's invitation?

Pray:

Almighty God, after the creation of the world you rested from all your works and declared a day of rest for all your creatures: Help us to put away our anxieties and prepare us to worship you without distraction and with our whole hearts. We come to you for protection and security, looking forward to the eternal rest promised in heaven; through Jesus Christ our Lord. Amen.

(Adapted from *Anglican Church in North America Book of Common Prayer*)

Seventh Sunday of Easter

KARI WEST

Read: *Psalm 147:1–11*

Praise the LORD!
For it is good to sing praises to our God;
for it is pleasant, and a song of praise is fitting.
The LORD builds up Jerusalem;
he gathers the outcasts of Israel.
He heals the brokenhearted
and binds up their wounds.
He determines the number of the stars;
he gives to all of them their names.
Great is our LORD, and abundant in power;
his understanding is beyond measure.
The LORD lifts up the humble;
he casts the wicked to the ground.
Sing to the LORD with thanksgiving;
make melody to our God on the lyre!
He covers the heavens with clouds;
he prepares rain for the earth;
he makes grass grow on the hills.
He gives to the beasts their food,
and to the young ravens that cry.
His delight is not in the strength of the horse,
nor his pleasure in the legs of a man,
but the LORD takes pleasure in those who fear him,
in those who hope in his steadfast love.

Reflect:

Do you look at the physical world and see the close, active love of God? These verses tell us that he is the one who pushes clouds into the sky, pours rain onto the earth, and pulls grass up from seeds to sprout on green hills. Ravens call to him for food, and he gives it to them. He numbers and names the stars in the heavens. All of creation is cultivated and cared for by his hand.

Take a moment to consider God's nearness and active love as shown in a world that continues to turn, in plants that break through the soil each spring, in newborn animals, in cloud-spread skies, and in life that is preserved and flourishing.

The care of God doesn't stop at the physical world. It crescendos, like a symphony, to the abiding, sustaining, specific love for his chosen people. He gathers his exiles; he binds their wounds and heals their broken hearts. He takes deep joy in those who honor him, and he sustains all those who are humble before him. On this side of the cross, we see that love culminating in the death and resurrection of Christ.

This psalm shows us how to respond to these beautiful realities. In humility, we can rely on our good God to provide what we need. We can come before him with awe at his transcendence and his power. We can put our hope in his unfailing love.

Does the sustaining love of God feel far from you? Speak this psalm out loud to the Lord in prayer. Ask for his Spirit to give you fresh insight into his perfect power, his tender care, and his abiding love for you.

Pray:

Father, you clothe the lilies, you feed the sparrows, and you sustain all life in the world, including mine. Thank you for your nearness and your care. Give me a spirit of humility and a heart that depends on you, for Jesus's sake. Amen.

Eastertide Day 44
BRANDON WALSH

Read: *Acts 1:15–26*

In those days Peter stood up among the brothers (the company of persons was in all about 120) and said, "Brothers, the Scripture had to be fulfilled, which the Holy Spirit spoke beforehand by the mouth of David concerning Judas, who became a guide to those who arrested Jesus. For he was numbered among us and was allotted his share in this ministry." (Now this man acquired a field with the reward of his wickedness, and falling headlong he burst open in the middle and all his bowels gushed out. And it became known to all the inhabitants of Jerusalem, so that the field was called in their own language Akeldama, that is, Field of Blood.) "For it is written in the Book of Psalms,

"'May his camp become desolate, and let there be no one to dwell in it';
and

"'Let another take his office.'

So one of the men who have accompanied us during all the time that the Lord Jesus went in and out among us, beginning from the baptism of John until the day when he was taken up from us—one of these men must become with us a witness to his resurrection." And they put forward two, Joseph called Barsabbas, who was also called Justus, and Matthias. And they prayed and said, "You, Lord, who know the hearts of all, show which one of these two you have chosen to take the place in this ministry and apostleship from which Judas turned aside to go to his own place." And they cast lots for them, and the lot fell on Matthias, and he was numbered with the eleven apostles.

Reflect:

The first order of business for the disciples after Jesus ascended was to replace Judas. Peter exhorted his fellow disciples that it must be someone who had been with Jesus from the baptism of John until his ascension. But notice the exact phrase he used: someone who "must become with us a witness to his resurrection" (v. 22).

This new disciple had to be a witness. The Greek word translated "witness" is from the same root as the word *martyr*. Acts depicts how the followers of Jesus, starting in Jerusalem and rippling outward to the ends of the earth, became witnesses to what the God of Israel had done through Christ.

This witness included preaching and proclamation, but by no means did it end there. Each of the main characters in Acts began to look like Jesus in their own flesh; they too became martyrs and witnesses. Their lives became little Christs (which is why they were first called "Christians"). Stephen, the first martyr recorded in the book of Acts, as he was stoned to death, asked the Lord not to hold the sin of his murderers against them. He then asked God to receive his spirit. These mirror the final words of Jesus as recorded in Luke.

All believers are called to become witnesses to Jesus's resurrection. Not only telling people about the good news of God in Christ but also becoming an announcement of that good news in our bodies. For some of us around the world, that looks much like the witness of Stephen. But all Christians must learn to lay down our rights and privileges so that we draw from Christ an identity that directs all the other aspects of our lives around his lordship.

As you pray, ask your Father to make you a witness to Jesus. Offer him your finances, your career, your politics, your sexuality. Submit to being crucified and resurrected so that your life will give testimony to his goodness, truth, and beauty.

Pray:

O God, you have made of one blood all the peoples of the earth, and sent your blessed Son to preach peace to those who are far off and to those who are near: Grant that people everywhere may seek after you and find you; bring the nations into your fold; pour out your Spirit upon all flesh; and hasten the coming of your kingdom; through Jesus Christ our Lord. Amen.

(Anglican Church in North America Book of Common Prayer)

Eastertide Day 45
KARI WEST

Read: *John 5:30–47*

"I can do nothing on my own. As I hear, I judge, and my judgment is just, because I seek not my own will but the will of him who sent me. If I alone bear witness about myself, my testimony is not true. There is another who bears witness about me, and I know that the testimony that he bears about me is true. You sent to John, and he has borne witness to the truth. Not that the testimony that I receive is from man, but I say these things so that you may be saved. He was a burning and shining lamp, and you were willing to rejoice for a while in his light. But the testimony that I have is greater than that of John. For the works that the Father has given me to accomplish, the very works that I am doing, bear witness about me that the Father has sent me. And the Father who sent me has himself borne witness about me. His voice you have never heard, his form you have never seen, and you do not have his word abiding in you, for you do not believe the one whom he has sent. You search the Scriptures because you think that in them you have eternal life; and it is they that bear witness about me, yet you refuse to come to me that you may have life. I do not receive glory from people. But I know that you do not have the love of God within you. I have come in my Father's name, and you do not receive me. If another comes in his own name, you will receive him. How can you believe, when you receive glory from one another and do not seek the glory that comes from the only God? Do not think that I will accuse you to the Father. There is one who accuses you: Moses, on whom you have set your hope. For if you believed Moses, you would believe me; for he wrote of me. But if you do not believe his writings, how will you believe my words?"

Reflect:

"How can you believe, when you receive glory from one another and do not seek the glory that comes from the only God?" (v. 44).

It is a terrifying possibility to contemplate: You can forfeit the glory of God, the riches of his presence, and the promise of the future inheritance of his saints because you prize a lesser thing—the praise of other people.

When this lesser thing is your highest goal and desire, you might study the Scriptures diligently and live a moral life but still miss everything in those Scriptures that points to the identity and supremacy of Jesus. And you will miss the great invitation that Christ holds out to follow him and thereby seek a higher glory.

It's an insidious thing—seeking and accepting glory from other people rather than seeking the glory of Christ. None of us who have been redeemed and who hold to Jesus as our Lord are immune to this temptation.

Sit with Christ's words and let the convicting power of the Spirit do its work. Do you truly believe that Jesus is Lord and worthy of glory, or have you been caught in the trappings of religion for your own elevation? Have you allowed your love of others' admiration to eclipse your desire for Christ's name to be lauded in all the earth?

As you pray, confess to your Savior and receive his full forgiveness. Thank him for these words and ask that his Spirit convict you and change you, molding your heart for the coming fullness of his presence, a splendor beyond imagining.

Pray:

What gratitude is justly due from me a sinner, who has been brought from darkness into light, and, I trust, from the pursuit of earthly things to the prime love of things above! O God, purify my heart still more by your grace. Quicken my dead soul, and purify me by your Spirit, that I may be changed from glory to glory, and be made even here in some degree to resemble my heavenly Father. Amen.

(William Wilberforce)

Eastertide Day 46

KARI WEST

Read: *John 6:27–40*

"Do not work for the food that perishes, but for the food that endures to eternal life, which the Son of Man will give to you. For on him God the Father has set his seal." Then they said to him, "What must we do, to be doing the works of God?" Jesus answered them, "This is the work of God, that you believe in him whom he has sent." So they said to him, "Then what sign do you do, that we may see and believe you? What work do you perform? Our fathers ate the manna in the wilderness; as it is written, 'He gave them bread from heaven to eat.'" Jesus then said to them, "Truly, truly, I say to you, it was not Moses who gave you the bread from heaven, but my Father gives you the true bread from heaven. For the bread of God is he who comes down from heaven and gives life to the world." They said to him, "Sir, give us this bread always."

Jesus said to them, "I am the bread of life; whoever comes to me shall not hunger, and whoever believes in me shall never thirst. But I said to you that you have seen me and yet do not believe. All that the Father gives me will come to me, and whoever comes to me I will never cast out. For I have come down from heaven, not to do my own will but the will of him who sent me. And this is the will of him who sent me, that I should lose nothing of all that he has given me, but raise it up on the last day. For this is the will of my Father, that everyone who looks on the Son and believes in him should have eternal life, and I will raise him up on the last day."

Reflect:

Do you hear the invitation in these words of Jesus? He declared that he is the bread of heaven who gives life to the world.

To believe in Jesus isn't an intellectual exercise in which we give a mental nod to certain facts about our Savior. It's an acknowledgment of that gnawing, constant hunger inside us and that deep desperation of knowing that we can't find true bread elsewhere. And it's an embracing of Jesus as the one and only person who holds out the true feast—himself.

Are you starving? Has your life revealed how little you can truly provide for yourself?

Go to Jesus. Embrace him as the only source of true life, and rest in his promise that he will never drive you away. He will keep you. He will hold you. He will love you. At the last day, he will raise you up to eternal life with him. His kingdom is inaugurated with a feast, the marriage supper of the Lamb. One day, that gnawing hunger you now know will be fully satisfied.

As you pray, ask for fresh faith to know—in your head and your heart and your bones and your stomach—that Jesus is the bread of life. He is all we need, and we are his forever.

Pray:
Jesus, you joy of living hearts!
You fount of life! You light of men!
From the best bliss that earth imparts,
We turn to you unfilled again. . . .
We taste you, O you living bread,
And long to feast upon you still;
We drink of you, the fountainhead,
And thirst our souls from you to fill.
Amen.

(Bernard of Clairvaux)

Eastertide Day 47

MADISON PERRY

Read: *John 14:1–7*

"Let not your hearts be troubled. Believe in God; believe also in me. In my Father's house are many rooms. If it were not so, would I have told you that I go to prepare a place for you? And if I go and prepare a place for you, I will come again and will take you to myself, that where I am you may be also. And you know the way to where I am going." Thomas said to him, "Lord, we do not know where you are going. How can we know the way?" Jesus said to him, "I am the way, and the truth, and the life. No one comes to the Father except through me. If you had known me, you would have known my Father also. From now on you do know him and have seen him."

Reflect:

For centuries, Christians buried their dead in the churchyard surrounding the church. One could not enter the church without seeing grave markers of generations clustered together—little children, young mothers, the aged. Those markers comforted the grieving as reminders that their loved ones were now gathered with the saints of all ages. Those markers spoke the truth we often avoid: Death comes for all.

Our world leaves dying to the experts. But what have we lost by not considering our own death? Would we live more fully, more humbly, and more wisely if we were to actively accept the reality that our time on this earth is brief? If we admit we too will die, will we care more deeply about those who will follow us?

God invites us to remember that we will all die. Have we entered into the forgiveness he offers us in Jesus Christ? Do we see the fragility of all life, and do we respect and esteem those around us? Do we need to remind ourselves that Jesus alone offers us eternal life? Do we need to ask if our lives will leave a blessing to those who follow us?

As you pray, consider whether you know that Jesus is the Good Shepherd who has laid down his life for you. Do you know he keeps you as you live and that he will keep you when you die? Thank your Shepherd Jesus that he is always with you. Pray for courage to live well and to die in faith, so that your living—and even your dying—might bring blessing to others. Remember that Christ has been resurrected and that we too will live in fullness beyond the grave.

Pray:

Lord Jesus, be mindful of your promise. Think of us, your servants, and when we shall depart, speak to our spirits these loving words: "Today you shall be with me in joy." O Lord Jesus Christ, remember us, your servants who trust in you, when our tongues cannot speak, when the sight of our eyes fails, and when our ears are stopped. Let our spirits always rejoice in you and be joyful about our salvation, which you through your death have purchased for us. Amen.

(Miles Coverdale)

Eastertide Day 48

GAYLE HEASLIP

Read: *3 John 2–12*

Beloved, I pray that all may go well with you and that you may be in good health, as it goes well with your soul. For I rejoiced greatly when the brothers came and testified to your truth, as indeed you are walking in the truth. I have no greater joy than to hear that my children are walking in the truth.

Beloved, it is a faithful thing you do in all your efforts for these brothers, strangers as they are, who testified to your love before the church. You will do well to send them on their journey in a manner worthy of God. For they have gone out for the sake of the name, accepting nothing from the Gentiles. Therefore we ought to support people like these, that we may be fellow workers for the truth.

I have written something to the church, but Diotrephes, who likes to put himself first, does not acknowledge our authority. So if I come, I will bring up what he is doing, talking wicked nonsense against us. And not content with that, he refuses to welcome the brothers, and also stops those who want to and puts them out of the church.

Beloved, do not imitate evil but imitate good. Whoever does good is from God; whoever does evil has not seen God. Demetrius has received a good testimony from everyone, and from the truth itself. We also add our testimony, and you know that our testimony is true.

Reflect:

How wonderfully encouraging it must have been for Gaius, in the midst of deceiving philosophies and opposition, to receive a letter from John.

The apostle had "no greater joy" (v. 4) than hearing about his friends' faithfulness to the truth of the gospel and their commitment to walking in the truth. Gaius was commended for the hospitality he offered to traveling evangelists who, though they were strangers to him, were received as those unified in the truth of Christ. They were each working toward the same goal of bringing eternal life to those who would receive it.

John also affirmed Gaius by contrasting him with a prideful church leader who refused to offer this hospitality. He cut off those under his authority and spread malicious rumors about the elders of area churches. He was divisive, impeding the gospel's radical access to the kingdom of God.

What matters most is fidelity to the truth of the gospel, walking in this truth, and offering oneself to it in word and deed. Gaius could rest in the security that what he did confirmed that he belonged to the Lord, for the Lord was the Author of his good actions.

Have you experienced a time when your actions of faithfully walking in the truth of the gospel brought conflict into your life? God sees your faithfulness and commitment to do what is good, and he commends you for it. He affirms that your life of faith comes from him. You bring him great joy as you offer him whatever you can, and as you can, unite with those who also bring the truth of Christ to others.

Will you receive his affirmation and offer yourself anew to serve this truth today? If there is one who comes to mind who also follows faithfully, you might send an encouraging note just as John did for Gaius.

Pray:

Heavenly Father, I can wither under oppression, feel overwhelmed by competing worldviews, and draw back from engagement. But how generous you are and how unending your resources! You invite me to commit to the truth of the gospel, living in it with confident expectation of your great joy in me as I continue to do what is good. May I not draw back from opportunities to do good but freely give what has been given to me by your generous hand, through Jesus Christ our Lord. Amen.

Eastertide Day 49
SALLY BREEDLOVE

Read: *Jude 17–25*

> But you must remember, beloved, the predictions of the apostles
> of our Lord Jesus Christ. They said to you, "In the last time there
> will be scoffers, following their own ungodly passions." It is these
> who cause divisions, worldly people, devoid of the Spirit. But you,
> beloved, building yourselves up in your most holy faith and praying
> in the Holy Spirit, keep yourselves in the love of God, waiting for
> the mercy of our Lord Jesus Christ that leads to eternal life. And
> have mercy on those who doubt; save others by snatching them out
> of the fire; to others show mercy with fear, hating even the garment
> stained by the flesh.
>
> Now to him who is able to keep you from stumbling and to
> present you blameless before the presence of his glory with great
> joy, to the only God, our Savior, through Jesus Christ our Lord, be
> glory, majesty, dominion, and authority, before all time and now
> and forever. Amen.

Reflect:

In this letter, Jude called himself the brother of James. Throughout the centuries, the church has believed that James was the half brother or perhaps first cousin of Jesus. If either case is true, then Jude knew Jesus intimately, long before he was revealed as the Son of God at the resurrection.

What would it have been like to be close kin with Jesus? When the family quarreled and hurt each other or disagreed about all the things families disagree about, Jesus would not have been involved in the fray. What about Jesus's perfect goodness made Jude marvel?

Jude learned from Jesus what it meant to be part of an imperfect family and yet not be caught up in the crisis. He passed on to us the truth he saw Jesus live out: We can mourn and yet not give up our outrage that the world is sinful and broken.

Jude invited us to attend to our own lives in God. He urged us to understand that a deepening faith doesn't simply happen; we choose practices that make room for faith to grow. We practice listening to the Spirit and praying alongside him. We choose to stay close to God's love. We put our hope in the mercy that will open the door to eternal life.

Jude called us to compassion toward fellow Christians. Have mercy on them, he said. Help them; don't judge them.

Finally, Jude shifted our attention beyond our own efforts to the incomparable Jesus. He is the one who keeps us, who is at work in us. He will one day present us with great joy to the Father.

Jude knew the truth: Jesus was not simply an amazing older brother or cousin. Jesus was Jude's Savior, the one he counted on. We too can count on Jesus.

As you pray, thank your Father in heaven that he is the one keeping you. Thank him for the security and joy he constantly offers you.

Pray:

O God, you made us in your own image, and you have redeemed us through your Son Jesus Christ: Look with compassion on the whole human family; take away the arrogance and hatred which infect our hearts; break down the walls that separate us; unite us in bonds of love; and work through our struggle and confusion to accomplish your purposes on earth; that, in your good time, all nations and races may serve you in harmony around your heavenly throne; through Jesus Christ our Lord. Amen.

(Anglican Church in North America Book of Common Prayer)

Pentecost Sunday
BRANDON WALSH

Read: *Acts 2:1–15*

When the day of Pentecost arrived, they were all together in one place. And suddenly there came from heaven a sound like a mighty rushing wind, and it filled the entire house where they were sitting. And divided tongues as of fire appeared to them and rested on each one of them. And they were all filled with the Holy Spirit and began to speak in other tongues as the Spirit gave them utterance.

Now there were dwelling in Jerusalem Jews, devout men from every nation under heaven. And at this sound the multitude came together, and they were bewildered, because each one was hearing them speak in his own language. And they were amazed and astonished, saying, "Are not all these who are speaking Galileans? And how is it that we hear, each of us in his own native language? Parthians and Medes and Elamites and residents of Mesopotamia, Judea and Cappadocia, Pontus and Asia, Phrygia and Pamphylia, Egypt and the parts of Libya belonging to Cyrene, and visitors from Rome, both Jews and proselytes, Cretans and Arabians—we hear them telling in our own tongues the mighty works of God." And all were amazed and perplexed, saying to one another, "What does this mean?" But others mocking said, "They are filled with new wine." But Peter, standing with the eleven, lifted up his voice and addressed them: "Men of Judea and all who dwell in Jerusalem, let this be known to you, and give ear to my words. For these people are not drunk, as you suppose, since it is only the third hour of the day."

Reflect:

Jesus told his disciples to wait, so they retreated from public view and prayed for something they really couldn't predict or understand. The disciples waited in Jerusalem, where many others from around the ancient world were assembled for the Feast of Pentecost.

For Jews, Pentecost celebrates the giving of the law of Moses and the beginning of the wheat harvest. God had promised to one day write his law in the hearts of his people. And at the first Pentecost after the resurrection, the Spirit came to rest on each one gathered. The same divine wind that the Lord breathed into Adam filled their lungs. As they spoke to the diverse crowds about what had happened, each listener heard Christ proclaimed in his or her own language.

This story might feel as foreign and startling to you as Moses parting the Red Sea or the burning bush. Likewise, the call of Christ can feel daunting, impossible even. How can we become like Christ? How can we be his witnesses? The Holy Spirit who fell on Pentecost, who animated the life and proclamation of the first apostles, is offered to us as well. The Holy Spirit lives in all who proclaim Christ as Lord. The same Spirit continues to work miracles in this world.

Pray that the Father will make you aware of the Holy Spirit in your life. Pray that the Spirit will be present in your hard conversations at work, around your family dinner table, and in your most important relationships. Invite the Holy Spirit to do in you what you cannot do in your own strength. Ask him to make you like Jesus. Ask the Spirit to blow through the church and bring in the harvest.

Pray:

Breathe in me, O Holy Spirit,
That my thoughts may all be holy.
Act in me, O Holy Spirit,
That my work, too, may be holy.
Draw my heart, O Holy Spirit,
That I love but what is holy.
Strengthen me, O Holy Spirit,
To defend all that is holy.
Guard me, then, O Holy Spirit,
That I always may be holy. Amen.

(Augustine of Hippo)

Acknowledgments

EIGHTH DAY PRAYERS has been the work of friends coming from a cross section of people, organizations, and churches who hope in the power of Scripture-focused prayer and hunger for the growth of God's church. This prayer guide would not be in print without Willa Kane's faith, generosity, and her ability to call people to action; Madison Perry's leadership, vision, and energy; Sally Breedlove's depth of spiritual insight and writing ability; and Kari West's love for Scripture and the written word.

But these four were not adequate for the work they felt called to. Cassie Lawrence offered her gift of meticulous copy editing, Isabel Yates brought an imagination for beauty and graphic design, and Alysia Yates took this project in hand with her immense skills as an editor and her ability to see the whole.

Eighth Day Prayers began with a simple idea that would have been impossible to execute without the enlivening help of the Holy Spirit. A friend of Willa's asked her if there was a way to call people to pray for eight minutes every night at 8:00 p.m. In 2020 our world was in a crisis of fear, isolation, and confusion, so how could a dream that big come into being? Willa, Madison, and Sally did the simple things. They named and set up a website and posted daily invitations to pray. From the beginning they realized prayer that flowed from reflection on Scripture had the power to draw people to the heart of God. They wrote the first 150 or so calls to prayer, and a growing number of people joined in online.

Out of that online worldwide community of over fourteen thousand people, the idea of a book began to emerge. And more people began to help with this project. Francis Capitanio gave significant creative direction, recommending the seasonal ordering and writing several entries along the way. Other writers for this volume include Phil Ashey, Steven E. Breedlove, Elizabeth Gatewood, Gayle Heaslip, and Brandon Walsh. Steven E. Breedlove also provided the rich introductions to the Christian year and the introductions to each season. Stephen Macchia graciously provided our introduction to what it means to reflect on Scripture in a prayer-filled way. The North

Carolina Study Center, a Christian study center based in Chapel Hill, North Carolina, devoted organizational assistance to bless the global church.

Psalm 110:3 tells us that God's people volunteer or offer themselves freely on the day of God's power. In the creation of *Eighth Day Prayers*, the triune God has indeed been our King, and his people have freely offered themselves in service. We are grateful.

About the Authors

Sally Breedlove is the author of *Choosing Rest* and one of the authors of *The Shame Exchange*. She is the cofounder of JourneyMates, a Christian soul care and spiritual formation ministry. She serves as a spiritual director and retreat leader and as associate director of Selah-Anglican, a spiritual direction training program. With her husband, Steve, a bishop in the Anglican Church in North America, she has ministered broadly across the United States, in Canada, and overseas. Sally is a mother to five and a grandmother to sixteen. She lives in Chapel Hill, North Carolina.

Willa Kane is a former trustee of The Anglican Relief and Development Fund and is presently a trustee of the American Anglican Council. She is one of the founders of New City Fellows, Raleigh, and a trustee for the ministries of Anne Graham Lotz. She was personally discipled by the late Michael Green in relational evangelism and in a commitment to care for the renewal and protection of the gospel on the global stage. For years, she has taught the Bible to women and mentored them. Together with her husband, John, she has poured her life into community leadership and development. Willa is a mother to four and a grandmother to twelve. She lives in Raleigh, North Carolina.

Madison Perry is the founder and executive director of the North Carolina Study Center, a Christian study center at UNC. He studied theology at Duke and law at UNC. An ordained priest in the Anglican Church in North America, his heart is to see university communities glorify the Lord and become places where young people are brought into God's kingdom, healed, and formed by the power of Jesus. He and his wife, Pamela, have six children and live in Durham, North Carolina. He enjoys talking while walking and reading all kinds of literature.

Alysia Yates is a writer, editor, and mother of four. She earned her graduate degree in church history and currently works as the project manager for Caritas Foundation International. Alysia has served as an ESL teacher within the refugee community, a facilitator for JourneyMates, and a mentor for the

New City Fellows Program. She lives with her husband, John, and two sons in Raleigh, North Carolina. She enjoys visiting her daughters at their universities, long walks with friends, and the delights of a good book.